# AUTISM QUESTIONS PARENTS ASK

## AUTISM HELP SERIES - BOOK ONE

## DR. SHARON A. MITCHELL

ASD PUBLISHING

As always, thanks to the wonderful editorial team of MEL. And, thanks to Katherine Munro for adding her perceptive edits.

This book is meant for informational purposes only. Discuss approaches with your therapists and use your own discretion. You know your child best.

Copyright © 2019 by Dr. Sharon A. Mitchell

ISBN 978-1-988423-05-0
All rights reserved.

No part of this book may be reproduced in any form or by any electronic or mechanical means, including information storage and retrieval systems, without written permission from the author, except for the use of brief quotations in a book review.

ALSO BY DR. SHARON A. MITCHELL

*Autism Goes to School*
*Autism Runs Away*
*Autism Belongs*
*Autism Talks and Talks*
*Autism Grows Up*
*Autism Questions Parents Ask*

And coming soon:

*Autism Questions Teachers Ask*
*The Autism Goes to School Workbook*
*Prequel to Autism Goes to School - Jeff's Story*
*Autism and the Dental Office*

## HOW TO USE THIS BOOK

If you have a child in your home, then likely life is not as orderly as you might have anticipated. This is especially true if that child has an autism spectrum disorder. That's okay. Being sequential is only one way to do things.

Time is likely a precious commodity for you. This book was designed with your life in mind. Most of the chapters in *Autism Questions Parents Ask* are short, meant to be read in those brief snatches of time you are able to carve out of your day.

While you are certainly welcome to begin at page one and read straight through, that is not necessary. Feel free to browse the table of contents and skip around to what interests you or what you are seeking at this moment.

The only exception to this might be the chapters that talk about sensory issues. If you are new to the concept of sensory sensitivities, you might want to begin with the chapter titled, <u>What is It with This Sensory Stuff?</u> Following that chapter you'll find sections detailing the eight sensory areas that might affect your child.

Pronouns are awkward and rather than continually using he/she throughout the book I have defaulted to generally using the male pronoun. While there are more diagnosed boys than girls, the use of "he" in no way implies that these autism characteristics apply only to males.

This book is by no means exhaustive and there is always a lot to learn about autism. At the back of this book you'll find the Endnotes section. There I've included links to where you can find out more information about topics we've discussed. The links lead to articles for those of you who like to read and to videos if you prefer to take in information that way. For those of you reading the e-book version, the links are clickable. If you have a paperback copy then check out the Endnotes section and you'll access all the same links.

If you find this book useful, you might also like its companion book, *Autism Questions Teachers Ask* that will be published September 15, 2019.

Check out the other books in the series:

*Autism Goes to School* [1]
*Autism Runs Away* [2]
*Autism Belongs* [3]
*Autism Talks and Talks* [4]
*Autism Grows Up* [5]
*Autism Questions Parents Ask* [6]

And coming soon:

*Autism Questions Teachers Ask* [7]
*The Autism Goes to School Workbook*
*Prequel to Autism Goes to School - Jeff's Story*
*Autism and the Dental Office*

## HOW CAN I HELP HIM?

*F*irst, do no harm. Well, that's a no-brainer for parents, right? No parent sets out to purposely harm their child.

What I mean by do no harm is that it is key to put your child first. He is more important than the advice of experts, your social standing or what family and neighbors think of him or of you.

You will receive advice from specialists that makes sense to you - it fits with your life philosophy and with what you know of your child. You will receive advice that does not sit so well with you, the needs of your family and what you feel are the needs of your child. Trust your instincts. You know your child the best and no one has his well-being at heart as much as you.

For many of us, the newly diagnosed autistic child is not the only kid in the family. The siblings have needs and are important as well. And, in many modern families both parents have jobs that contribute to the family's economic well-being. There are only so many hours in a day.

I know of parents who have felt pressured to take out a second mortgage on their home to pay for "required" treatment for their child. There are fear-mongers who, while perhaps with good intentions, tell parents that there is this tiny window - a small period of time when their child's mind is open to intervention so it is crucial to do whatever it takes to give that toddler or preschooler 40 hours of intensive one-on-one interventions every week.

Think about that. While your little one may have an autism diagnosis, he is still a child - a small child.

How do other preschoolers learn? How did your other children learn? Did they pick up skills only through structured lessons and formal interactions that last as long as most adults spend at work?

Yes, your child with autism is different. He wouldn't even have this diagnosis if he learned in the same way as do others his age. That is true. But, he is still a child. Kids learn through play. (It is not the purpose of this book to espouse one form of therapy over another, although my bias is toward play-based approaches).

This is a cautionary reminder to take into account not only the needs of the newly diagnosed child, but your other children and the family as a whole. If the treatment option you pick destroys your family financially, have you created a whole host of other problems that will impact each and every person in your household?

YOU HAVE OPTIONS. If the initial advice you receive seems like too much, too expensive or your gut tells you that it's not a fit for your child and family, seek other options. There are lots.

Professionals may have studied autism; you have studied your son or daughter and are experts on them. Trust your gut.

WHEN LOOKING for advice an excellent source are those articulate, autistic adults who are willing to share with you their insights. When you wonder just what is going on inside your child's mind, what his take on the situation might be, what things might have upset him, turn to those adults who have been there.

There are lots of them once you know where to look. On Twitter, seek out the hashtag #askingautistics. You find a generous group of autistics there who willingly reflect back on what life was like for them at your child's age. Another great source is a Facebook group called Autism Inclusivity[7], set up by autistic adults willing to answer questions and offer guidance to parents.

What these adults commonly hear is, "But you're not like my child." Of course, they aren't! They're adults. While at age four some of them might have been nonverbal, as they aged, they acquired communication skills, just as your child will. Their adult self may look drastically different than your four-year-old son or daughter, but when that adult was four, the differences might have been miniscule.

They will never be identical, however. Each person is an individual with unique patterns of strengths, struggles and interests, so while you may not find an adult who is "just like" your child, you will find some who have more in common with your child than do your child's siblings or even with you. Learn from these people; listen to them. Their insights will help you and your child tremendously.

When you're trained to study arachnids (spiders) then every bug someone points out you first see through the possible spider lens. When you are trained exclusively in one autism therapeutic approach, you tend to see all autistic kids as fitting into or requiring the only kind of therapy you know. Really though, is there just one way to do anything? I'm a teacher and I teach soon-to-be-teachers in university. There is not just one way to teach children how to read. There are a myriad of approaches, some more suitable to some kids than others. (More on this in the next chapter). If you canvass every adult on your street, querying how they learned to drive, you will receive a multitude of answers and stories and methods. That is simply a fixture of the way we learn.

And, how we learn is not a stagnant thing. For some subjects and at some stages in your life you might learn best by reading or by listening or by doing. It changes depending on your needs and skills at the moment. That is the same with our children. There may be parts of one type of therapy that you feel suit the current needs but then you feel that something else better suits other concerns or circumstances. You do not need to put all your pennies in one bucket - you get to choose and change your mind and weave a course that best matches your child.

If you run into a specialist who tells you that there is only ONE approach that will ever work for an autistic child, run. Well, maybe don't literally run, but take that with a grain of salt.

Step back and think it through before you commit yourself and your child. Through what lens is that person speaking? What will they get out of it? How broad is their knowledge beyond that one approach? What are other people doing? What do adult autistics have to say about this?

Don't write anyone off but don't take at face value what they say, either. And, about that "window" of time and the fear that it might be closing before you take action, dooming your child forever? Pshaw. Seriously. Don't believe it. Sure, kids do acquire knowledge and skills rapidly during the preschool years. But a hallmark of autistic kids is that they step to their own drummer and learn at their own pace.

Did YOU stop learning after age 6? At my advanced age of 40 I began taking piano lessons. At the even more advanced age of 50 I began and completed a PhD program. Now, a decade later, I've taken up welding. Learning does not stop.

The window does not and will not close on your child. Relax. Take a deep breath. You have time and your child has time. Seriously.

When you begin to think about therapies, may I add a cautionary note? Don't aim to *change* your child. We so clearly hear from autistic adults the damage from the message that they are wrong, broken, in need of fixing; that their instinctive likes, methods of soothing themselves and sources of enjoyment are wrong or bad. Please, don't give your child that message.

Instead aim for giving your child skills that will help him or her navigate the more challenging areas of his life. Your goal is not to change your child into something he is not, but to help him grow into the best self he can be by celebrating his strengths and giving him tools to handle the areas that are hard for him.

And, never assume. This is key. Never talk about your child in front of him, thinking that he can't hear you or doesn't understand. Likely he can hear and does understand even if he does not say so. Always presume competence. We hear horror stories from autistic adults about things people said to and about them. Do a YouTube search for people like Amanda Baggs[8] and listen to what she has to say through the use of text-to-voice technology.

YOUR CHILD MIGHT BE a kid with an autism diagnosis, but he is a kid. As such, much of what he does will be colored through his autistic lens of the world. That's a given. But what's also a given is that he is a kid. Sometimes kids are angelic and sometimes they might even be naughty. Yep, even your angel.

All children need guidance and structure. The latter is particularly important for autistic kids. Partly due to their neurology, autistic children have a hard time making sense of the world. The routines that your other children simply pick up through osmosis might still remain a mystery to your autistic kid. You can help by creating routines and schedules. This is the pattern we always follow in the morning. How that pattern will look depends on your household. For instance, your child might wake up and go to the bathroom. In the bathroom, his routine might be to use the toilet, wash his hands and face, brush his teeth, etc. While you might initially guide him through these steps, believe me, it will make life easier for all of you if you create a visual schedule on the wall depicting (in words [if he can read] or pictures) what he is to do and the order in which he should do them. Having the visual schedule saves you from repeating yourself over and over (which becomes suspiciously like nagging) and fosters independence in your child.

Next, have a similar schedule in the bathroom for the order in which you want him to get dressed. There could be a visual schedule on your fridge for what he is to do in the kitchen for breakfast, etc. This cuts down on the amount of talking you'll have to do and builds on skills of doing more for himself. Autistic kids take information that they see more readily than that which they hear, especially during times of anxiety or upset. Visual schedules are your friend. Trust me on this. Just as your child will benefit from being able to count on your love and on your routines, so will he benefit from expectations. Yes, expectations.

He may be autistic, but he's still a member of the family and as such will contribute to the running of the household. Of course, that participation is strictly dependent on age and skill level, but even small children can help. When he removes his dirty socks in the evening, do they lay on the floor where they've fallen? A two-year-old can learn to throw his dirty garments in the laundry hamper. That same child can help set the table if there is a paper/placement that outlines where the plate, cup and cutlery should go. Chores are age-specific and skill specific, but it helps if a child has expectations, no matter how minute.

Yes, even autistic kids. Do you feel sorry for your child? Don't go there. It's not your fault and it's not his fault that he is autistic. It just is. It's now your job to help him grow into the best Johnny he can be and that includes being responsible even in just small ways.

Now, will he want to throw his dirty clothing in the laundry hamper? Doubtful. Who does if someone will come along and do it for you? He might be especially reluctant if he spots his beloved building blocks in the corner.

Try a First_____, Then_____ approach. In words, or better yet in pictures, clearly but firmly demonstrate that first you put the dirty socks in the hamper then you get to play with the block or whatever else is his preferred activity. Honestly, this is good training for this week, this year, for school and for life.

And now for the most important thing you can do for your child. Love him. I know you already do but do it even more and unconditionally. Let him know how much you adore him just the way he is and accept and cherish him. Again, that message comes through loud and clear from autistic adults - how important it is to feel that you are loved and accepted, that you aren't regarded as broken in need of fixing.

## WHAT KIND OF THERAPIES ARE OUT THERE?

When you're new to autism, you might madly scour the internet in search of help. Please keep in mind that there is no *one* way for help every autistic person. As mentioned in the previous chapter, make sure you choose an approach that suits *your* child and *your* family and your child's current needs. Trust your gut. Go with what feels right. (And know that there are autistic kids who grew up to be okay autistic adults without any formal therapy at all).

If you're looking for treatment options, there are lots. We'll look at just a few that you'll come across. These are listed in alphabetical order.

### ABA

When you begin your research into therapies, you will hear about ABA[9] (applied behavior analysis) or IBI (intensive behavior intervention). We'll devote more time to this approach because it is widely used and might be recommended to you. It is based on the work of psychologists B.F. Skinner and Ivar Lovaas from the 50s and 60s. Over the years a gentler approach to ABA has evolved where the use of cattle prods and electric shocks is mostly frowned on now. If ABA is your choice, make sure that the therapist is a good fit for your child and for your family's values. Think about how your child will generalize these skills in the real world without an adult there to prompt or reward him. Depending on the philosophy and training of the ABA therapist, there is a big difference, so shop around and choose carefully since you know your child best.

Although ABA is the approach you might hear of most often when you research autism, please beware that there is controversy about it. Many of the criticisms come from autistic adults who received ABA as children. Here are a few of their thoughts:

- What I Liked and (Didn't Like) About My ABA Experience[1]
- What's the Big Deal with ABA Therapy?[2]
- The Controversy Over Autism's Most Common Therapy[3]

- A Balanced View of ABA by An Autistic Adult [4]
- Does ABA Harm Autistic People? [5]
- How I Teach Autistic Students Without Using ABA [6]

ONE CAVEAT. When some parents hear the criticisms of the ABA therapy their child receives, they say that that is not *my* ABA. Maybe yes and maybe no. For the most part, ABA is non- regulated. There are various training institutions that will offer ABA certification but there is no universal standard. The amount/type of training the therapist has varies widely.

In some areas, ABA is the only therapy covered by health insurance. Some therapy providers admit that they are not trained ABAers and don't actually deliver ABA treatment, but they call it ABA or IBI so that the costs will be covered.

Carefully consider the pros and cons of ABA (and of any approach) and don't sign up for a therapy because you think there are no alternatives.

### DIETARY INTERVENTIONS

Not all, but many autistic kids experience

gut issues. These may include things such as chronic diarrhea, constipation, bloating, gas, abdominal distension, fecal impaction, gastro-esophageal reflux, leaky gut syndrome, etc. Their nutritional requirements might not always be met due restricted self-selection in what they will eat, based on sensory sensitivities.

These medical conditions need to be investigated by a physician. Often kids don't tell us when they are in physical discomfort; this is especially true when this condition is chronic for the child and all he or she has ever known.

For some kids, dietary changes[7] can bring some relief to these symptoms. The most common one you will find is a gluten-free/casein-free diet[8]. Gluten is a protein in wheat and casein is a protein in dairy products. After trying this diet for a number of months, some parents report a lessening of their child's symptoms. It is not easy, though to remove all gluten and casein from the foods a child eats and there is concern about ensuring that there is adequate calcium in the child's diet. Due to the GF/CF[9] diet or the child's narrow range of tolerated foods, there can be concerns about nutritional deficiencies and supplements might be warranted. A pediatrician, dietician or nutritionist may offer good guidance.

One caution when you are looking into dietary approaches. Please do not feed your child bleach[10]. Yes, bleach. There are some sellers who claim that if your child ingests their bleach product or (shudder) you give him bleach enemas that his autism will be cured.

**Early Start Denver Model**

The Early Start Denver Model[11] is relationship-based and involves the family. Their goals are to improve the child's language, cognitive and social abilities and use the principles of ABA.

**Floortime**

If a play-based approach suits you and your child, there are numerous options. One of the best known is Stanley Greenspan's Floortime[12] approach. (You can watch part of a Floortime session and learn more about it here[13].

MORE THAN WORDS

If communication is your main concern, look into the Hanen approach *More Than Words*[14]. Its focus is on communication rather than just eliciting spoken responses and teaches parents ways to help their children communicate. You can see it in action at https://www.youtube.com/watch?v= W189Mb-2FnM[15].

### Picture Exchange Communication System

The Picture Exchange Communication System (PECS)[16] has the goal of independent communication. It is used with nonverbal or minimally verbal people and through graduated lessons teaches how to use pictures to communicate wants and needs, using the principles of ABA.

### PRT

Somewhat akin to ABA is PRT, Pivotal Response Treatment[17]. While having its roots there and following some ABA principles, it revolves around things that mean a lot to your child and developing positive interactions. Some describe PRT as a more naturalistic ABA. There was a *SuperNanny*[18] episode that demonstrates this.

### Rapid Prompting

Rapid Prompting[19] is a method devised by Soma Mukhopadhyay, a mom of a nonverbal autistic child. It's a way of helping a nonverbal child learn to communication by pointing to letters to spell out his thoughts. You can watch a demonstration here[20].

### Reference and Regulate

REFERENCE AND REGULATE'S[21] philosophy is "learn to look, look to learn". Many kids on the autism spectrum do not make eye contact with others in a fashion typical to others their age. There may be lots of reasons for this, including neurological differences that make eye contact uncomfortable.

One of the reasons we look at people's faces is to glean information. Autistic kids are often poor at reading body language and facial expressions. There is speculation as to whether this is because they have gathered less experience with this because that type of looking is uncomfortable or that when they look, they get little out of it so have learned not to bother.

A Reference and Regulate therapist will never say to a child, "Look at me." Nor do they encourage parents to do so either. Instead, through play that the child enjoys, eye contact develops naturally as a way to get the therapist (or parent) to do what the child wants and to have shared enjoyment.

### RDI

Relationship Development Interventions[22] is another. It has similarities to Floortime. (This link[23] will give you a taste of what this approach is about).

Both of these, as do many others, involve

parent interactions. This is different than having a trained professional come into your home 20 or 40 hours a week to deliver therapy to your child. Parent involvement approaches certainly do have trained professionals as key participants, but often they demonstrate and guide parents in interactions with the child. After all, who spends the most time with the child? Parents and siblings. Just by the sheer volume of hours alone, the parent has the largest influence in the child's life.

**SCERTS**

The SCERTS Model[24] stresses social communication, self-regulation and transactional support. Its goal is to help autistic kids become confident and competent social communicators. It's an approach that stresses the team of support - parents, educators and therapists. It attempts to fit into the lives of the participants, is relevant to not just young children, can form the basis of home and school plans and can incorporate other approaches.

### Sensory Integration Therapy

Sensory Integration Therapy[25] is usually conducted by an occupational therapist. Most

OTs have a Master's degree plus additional training in sensory integration.

Like most of the therapies listed in this chapter, sessions will be geared to your child. Although it's work, kids often find their appointments to be fun. Check out What You Should Know about Sensory Integration Therapy[30].

It is a rare autistic child (or adult) who does not have some difficult with sensory modulation. This is a big enough topic that we'll devote half a dozen chapters to it later on in this book.

Along with possibly being over- or under-aroused in some sensory areas, some autistic kids struggle with fine and/or gross motor control, balance and coordinating movements. OTs[31] work on these issues as well.

While not all OTs are formally trained in sensory integration therapy, OTs can help autistic kids in many ways. Here's an article on *Top Ways Occupational Therapy Can Help Kids With Autism Every Day*[26].

### Son Rise

Son Rise[27] is another method to consider. But again, I would caution you about any program that talks about "recovery" or "cure". You can watch a session here[28].

. . .

## Speech Therapy

When you hear the words "speech therapy[29]" you might think of, well, speech. The actual act of speaking is only part of what a speech therapist will work on. (We go into more detail on speech in the chapters Will He Ever Talk? And What If He Never Talks?).

Speech therapy is conducted by a Speech and Language Pathologist (called Speech and Language Therapist in the UK). An SLP usually has a Master's degree.

SLPs work on far more than just speech; they consider all aspects of language and communication. Autism is often called a social communication disorder and those skills fall within the realm of an SLP's experience.

Social skills can include such things as turn-taking, sharing, requesting, joining a group, reciprocity (the give and take of conversation), etc.

SLPs are concerned with not only *how* a child forms words (articulation) but how the child communicates (sends and receives messages). If a child is nonverbal or minimally verbal (see later chapters on these topics) they will help the child find ways to communicate his wants and needs.

## TEACCH

TEACCH[30] stands for the Treatment and Education of Autistic and related Communication-handicapped Children therapeutic methodology. Here's some information on TEACCH[31].

THE ABOVE LIST is by no means exhaustive; it is simply meant to show you that there are options that you need to consider and match to your child, his/her needs, your life and your philosophy.

# WHICH PROFESSIONALS MIGHT HELP US?

Once the reality of a diagnosis sinks in there is often a mad dash to find the professionals who can help. Spoiler alert - no matter how hard you look, no matter how much money you spend or who you find to be on your team, no one can make the autism go away. Seriously. If someone tells you that they can "cure" your child of autism, run and run fast. Either that person is purposely trying to mislead you, sell you false hope or they really don't know much about autism.

Autism is a life-long condition, a way of viewing and interacting with the world. This basic neurology will not go away.

But there are things that can be done to make life easier for your child. That is what you might seek from professionals.

Let's look at who might be in your corner. Autism is a social communication disorder.

This applies to every autistic kid, even those who seem to be highly verbal as well as those who are not speaking at all. A group of professionals you might find useful are speech/language therapists. For just a minute, we'll discuss some of the titles they might go by:

- speech/language therapist (SLT)
- speech/language pathologist (SLP) - speech therapist
- language therapist
- speech and language therapist (SALT)

In North America, the title speech/language pathologist (SLP) is commonly used: in Britain, speech and language therapist (SALT) is heard frequently.

A speech/language pathologist is someone who has spent a number of years at university or college - often at least 5 years. They might have taken undergraduate classes in language development, psychology, child development, neurology, physiology, anatomy, etc. while getting their Bachelor's Degree. In most countries this is not enough education to be a practicing speech/language therapist and they must take a couple years more training to get their Master's degree. Some will carry on attaining doctorate degrees although that is less common. These years at school focus on typical speech and language development, atypical development, acquired communication difficulties (such as through head injuries, strokes, etc.), social communication, pragmatics, assistive technology, apraxia and articulation, to just name a few of the areas. Some SLTs branch off into audiology where they specialize in the assessment of hearing and auditory processing. Their university training includes practical, supervised experience and as well as internships before being licensed to practice.

When you mention the words speech therapist what sometimes come to mind is an adult working with a child who says "wabbit" for "rabbit". This is an articulation error and something that an SLP might work on. Some people are surprised when an SLP does not get all bent out of shape about a small child's lisp or articulation error. Some such errors are not unusual in kids of a certain age. At this link[1] you can find information on the speech sounds and language skills that are typical for various ages.

SLPs work on both speech and language. Speech is how we say words and encompasses such things as articulation, fluency and voice. Although the speech area is the one we might be most familiar with, SLPs also focus on language. Language is divided into two main areas - receptive and expressive, meaning how we take in language and how we express our wants, needs and ideas. On this page[2] you'll find an explanation of both speech and language. Your child might be showing struggles in one or both of these areas. It is common for autistic kids to have language difficulties.

Another area that SLPs might work on is social skills or social understanding. They are not the only discipline that is knowledgeable in this area. Psychologists, occupational therapists, counsellors and educators also work on social understanding. This is a good thing that so many professionals take an interest in social understanding for it is a realm full of challenges for autistic individuals.

ANOTHER PROFESSIONAL WHO might help is an occupational therapist. Like SLPs, these are therapists have spent at least 5 or 6 years in training at university, including internships in various settings. OT's can assist in a variety of ways. Here's what the Canadian Association of Occupation Therapists has to say about their work:

An occupational therapist will try to find out why a client cannot do what they would like or need to do. An OT may check:

• your physical abilities like strength, balance and coordination,

- your mental abilities like memory, coping strategies, organizational skills
- what materials or devices you use to participate in activities like furniture, utensils, tools or clothes,
- which social and emotional support is available to you at home, school, work or in the community, and
- the physical setup of your house, classroom, workplace or other environment.

SOME OTs HAVE additional training focused on sensory issues. We discussed sensory challenges earlier in this book. An OT can be helpful in identifying which sensory areas may be impacting your child's life and where he is under-responsive or over-responsive. They can also help the child cope with these challenges, reduce some of the extremes and help him or her to better self-regulate.

This is huge! Many of the behaviors that are most troubling could have a sensory basis and any help you can get in this area will be very welcome.

OTs also assist with the tasks of daily living - everything from eating to dressing to using the bathroom and navigating their world. Although every OT practice differs, here's a short video clip[3] of how one OT group works with kids and families.

Psychologists might also play a part in helping your child. These professionals have either a Master's level or Doctorate level degree in their field. Psychologists are often involved in the diagnostic process. Part of the diagnostic criteria specifies whether or not the child also has an intellectual disability; this is the domain of a psychologist. But their role need not end with simply an IQ test.

Anxiety is something that plagues many autistic children and adults. They might even have a separate diagnosis of anxiety disorder. The anxiety might stem from sensory issues, understanding the social world, feeling different or trying to fit into their world, etc. But it's still anxiety and if you have ever experienced anxiety, it is not pleasant to say the least. A psychologist might be one of the professionals who would help your child learn ways to manage anxiety. They might do it through desensitization, cognitive behavior therapy, relaxation techniques, build on the child's social understanding or many other ways that would be appropriate to that particular child. The therapist might also work with you on ways to parent an anxious child.

Psychologists might also look at adaptive functioning - how well your child manages in his world compared to others his age. Kids who have intellectual disabilities are usually behind their peers in the self-help and independence areas of adaptive functioning. But some bright autistic children may also lag in adaptive functioning or have scattered results where they are on par with the peers (or even above them) in some areas but be delayed in others.

These adaptive functioning skills are things that an occupational therapist or a psychologist may help with.

You might think that there is some overlap, and you would be right. Psychologists, OTs and/or SLPs might all run groups or individual sessions that build your child's skills in understanding the social world. Some might be called social skills groups; others work more on social understandings to help your child navigate his world.

SOCIAL WORKERS ARE another group who might offer some assistance. While there are social workers whose jobs focus on child protection and some on financial aid, others fill counselling roles. They might work independently with your child or on a team with some of these other professionals.

THERE ARE large groups of people who call themselves therapists or counsellors. Depending on where you live, some will be licensed and some not. Some will have university training in their field; some will have training in varying lengths from a weekend course to several years of study in one particular approach.

A word of caution here. Get references. Are other parents pleased with the results when this person/organization worked with their child? Is there data- driven evidence that this approach works? What is the cost? If they are asking you to take out a second mortgage on your house, be leery.

Do they promise a cure? If so, run. Autism is not something that goes away. Your child will learn and grow and acquire skills, but he will always be autistic, even when daily functioning becomes easier. Do they promise that by a certain age he will be "indistinguishable from his peers"? Again, the autism will not go away.

Does the approach respect your child for who he is as a person? Will he be made to feel badly about his natural likes and inclinations? Does it just want to change him? Will this approach fit into your family's lifestyle, beliefs and budget? Is there the potential for physical harm? Mental harm? Is it developmentally appropriate? Think about how other kids his age learn. Is it natural for a three-year-old to sit at a table for eight hours a day? Children learn through play and they learn best when they feel loved and accepted.

DESPITE THE MYRIAD of professionals who might offer you assistance, you will not be taking your child to someone else who will "fix him". He's autistic; that won't go away and that's okay. What you are looking for are ways to help your child be more comfortable in his environment, be better able to manage himself, to follow his dreams and to thrive. How is that different for what you want for any of your children?

# WHAT SHOULD I NOT DO?

Before having children, you might have thought that kids would fit into your life quite easily. Hah! Little did you know that you would be at the mercy of these tiny new beings.

You recovered from that initial shock. Then you expected your bundle of joy to follow the trajectory set out in all those baby books. If your child has an autism diagnosis, you will likely have noticed that he forges ahead at his own pace.

That is a fact and you cannot change it. Oh, you can love and guide and teach and organize and comfort but you cannot change who he is. To attempt to do so leads to heartbreak both for you and for your child.

If that child is autistic, he is different. Get over it; he just is. Trying to form him into a mould of your choosing will not work.

Think of those events and activities you tried to make him enjoy that ended in disaster. What caused things to go awry? Was it your child misbehaving or was it a parent trying to force the child to be something he isn't? That might sound harsh, but it happens all too often.

Are you trying to force your child to tolerate something that is currently too much for him?

You might believe that all children love parades and insist that your autistic child join you. While *some* might find it truly entertaining, for others the assault on their senses might be too much to bear, causing a meltdown. Think about those factors that make the day exciting for some. There is the sun, the wind and the temperature on your skin. There are the crowds and the buzz of excitement. People might brush by you; they might chat with you. There can be endless waiting since you arrived early to get a front-row spot. Then in the distance you can hear the approaching. The wail of the trumpets and cornets, the tinkling glockenspiel, the pounding of the bass drum as they approach. Does your child have sensory sensitivities? The encroaching noises could actually be painful to him. As the noise gets closer and his tension builds to a distressing level, he cries and screams in terror. Now, is it his fault that the trip to the parade has been ruined or was he placed in a situation that would be too much for him?

LISTEN TO YOUR CHILD; learn to read his body's signs. Choose activities that will suit him rather than trying to force him to be someone he isn't. That is not to say that he should not be exposed to new things - for sure he should be but think about them from his point of view and gear him for success.

A few years ago, there was a flurry of news and social media attention on "Elmo mom", a caring mother who felt that her son should enjoy concerts and get over his fear of unknown indoor spaces. Read the mom's version[1] of the incident then what autistic adults suggest[2] [3].

You may be more inclined to agree with one side of the other or fall squarely in the middle. How you comport yourself and what you expect of your child needs to be based on your knowledge and understanding of that child, his skills and current challenges.

"Not an Autism Mom" runs a blog. One of her excellent posts is called, *Autism Did Not Ruin the Event. My Own Expectations Did*[4]. It is well worth your read.

Fighting to make the autistic parts of your

child disappear won't work and the stress to you and your child will be sizeable. Andrea Libutti, a physician and mom of an autistic boy wrote a nice blog about this. *Autism: Tragedy or Blessing*[5].

Parenting can be a daunting challenge at the best of times but it's even harder when that child is autistic. The child did not come with a manual and worse, just when you think you have things figured out, something changes.

But what will not change is that your child is autistic. He will definitely grow and learn but the basic neurology that is autism will always remain.

Like all parents, there will be times when you just need an ear, a sympathetic listener who has been there, who gets it. Please seek that someone carefully. In this age of online presence, there can be a tendency to "over-share" with those faceless strangers on the internet.

Remember that anything posted online remains there, accessible forever. If you post naked your three-year-old, those pictures will be available when your son is twenty-five. Think about how your older child will feel about pictures or descriptions you once posted of him online.

Please don't do these things:

- post pictures of your child in a meltdown on social media
- post pictures of damage your child has done to your home
- post pics/details of your child's toileting on social media
- don't describe your "grief" upon hearing of your child's diagnosis
- don't say your child is ruining your life
- don't say "I hate autism" because autism is intrinsic to your child and it sounds like you then hate *him*
- don't believe that by the age of 3 or 4 your child's whole life path is determined.

ALTHOUGH AUTISM WILL COLOR your child's view of the world, not every single thing is about autism. He or she is still a kid. Kids mess up; they want their own way and don't always make the best choices. Yes, sometimes his response will be from an autism perspective but sometimes he might display naughty behavior that is just being a kid. It might not always be easy to discern which it is, but he does not get a pass on inappropriate behavior because he is autistic. Like any child he will still need rules and guidance.

I sometimes hear parents complain about their child's school. They say that they don't see any of those behaviors at home and he'd be fine at school if they just let him do what he wanted to do. While that *might* work at home, in group situations it just doesn't. Most definitely the school needs to understand and accommodate his needs but that is not the same as having no expectations of him.

We all need down time, but no one gets to just do exactly as they please all the time. How would that type of catering help your child later in life? The world does not work that way. A child, autistic or not, needs rules, routines and responsibilities appropriate to his maturity level.

# WHY DID THIS HAPPEN TO US?

*A*h, this is something parents ask a lot, especially those with a newly diagnosed child.

First, it's not your fault. You did nothing to cause this difference in your child. It happens.

Still, it is a difference and you suspect that autism will make you child's life harder than it would be if he wasn't autistic. No one wants things to be hard for their child. Take time (just a bit of time) to grieve. Yes, life might look different than the path shown in your dreams. But different can be okay and it will be okay. Emily Perl Kingsley wrote a poem[1] about this.

SINCE AUTISM IS SO PREVALENT, a lot of effort

and funds are going into the possible etiologies or causes of autism. Most agree that there is a genetic component to autism. While not directly inheritable, there is a stronger incidence within some families. If one child has autism there is a higher than average chance that a sibling will also show signs of autism. The rate varies study to study, but if you are interested, here is an article that will give you more information and links for further studies[2]. It's not the easiest article to wade through but offers good information.

If you hear that autism has a genetic basis, often we think of something inherited. But, "if you have one child with autism, the risk for the next child is only 2 - 6%. If autism were due to a single gene, we might expect numbers like 25% or 50%." The article at this link[3] is an easier read. It talks about some of the genetic studies done with families who have and don't have children who are on the autism spectrum. In some cases, the children share the same genetic abnormalities of their parents, even when the parent does not have a diagnosis. Other times the child's genetic pattern shows a duplication or gene deletion.

Either way, this is not something you as a parent or potential parent could control.

**Is this something from his dad's side of the family?**

Don't go there. You will never know

which possible genetic combinations might have resulted in or contributed to your child's autism. Now is not the time for the blame game. It's done and there was nothing you could have done to prevent it. Your child needs your full support now and a united family is a gift you can give him or her.

**But Why?**

There are several schools of thought about the research into the cause of autism. Some people would like to know what causes autism so that it can be prevented from happening. Many parents are in this camp - it hurts to see your child struggle and we'd all like life to be as smooth as possible for our children.

Other people feel that there is only so much money to go around. It's a fact that we have autistic kids. Rather than funding research into a cause, they would rather that money go toward effective treatments to make life easier for the kids and for their families.

HERE'S one way of thinking - *if you can't make it not happen, make it go away.*

While you might have some sympathy for wanting it all to just go away, especially on those bad days, articulate, autistic adults take great exception to this. Think about it. Trying to eradicate autism makes it seem like you are trying to get rid of those who *are* autistic. What value are you putting on their lives? There are many autistic adults who are happy. They like themselves. Sure, most freely admit to the struggles they have had and still do have, but they think they are okay.

Put yourself in their shoes (or in the shoes your child will one day wear). Autism in many ways defines their lives; it is not an add-on to their way of being - it *is* their way of being. Then listen to people wanting to stamp out autism, to eradicate it from this world. Imagine how that would feel. (Like it's a form of genocide). Now you might understand the resentment many autistic adults hold for those organizations they perceive as wishing to banish their existence from the face of this earth. How does that jibe with those autistic adults who like themselves, who enjoy their life, despite their struggles and feel that they have something to offer the world?

The wanting-it-to-go-away at all costs has led to some potentially dangerous practices. Think long and hard about having your child ingest substances that are reported to "cure" autism.

SOME PARENTS MIGHT SAY, "My child will never be like those adults." Perhaps, but who knows? Never assume. The way your child is at age 3 will resemble little about the adult he will become. Who knows how he will develop? Do not write him off and do not set limits on his growth.

Yeah, easier said than done. It's hard when all the other kindergarten kids are running around, chatting to friends and approaching each new task with enthusiasm, but your child does not want to leave your side. He does not speak. He does not appear to even notice the other students.

Again, don't assume. Just because it does not look like he is aware of his surroundings does not mean that he is oblivious. In fact, he may be hyper-aware, taking in everything at once with an intensity the rest of us could only imagine. His little body could be bombarded with input he is struggling to manage without being totally overwhelmed.

It's tough when a child does not talk - tough on his family and teachers but even tougher on him. But not being able to speak is not the same thing as not having anything to say.

Yes, speech is likely the easiest and most direct way to communicate but when this option is not available, there are other ways. Many parents of nonverbal kids develop a sixth sense as to what their child seeks. Most develop elaborate systems of pantomiming, pointing and trial and error. Frustrating for you? Yep. Frustrating for the child? We can only imagine. We'll go into communication more in the chapter Will He Ever Talk.

Please, please, do not talk about your child in front of him. Some people assume that because a child does not talk, he cannot understand your words.

Autism happens. It's no one's fault. Get over it and get on with it.

# SHOULD WE TELL HIM HE HAS AUTISM/IS AUTISTIC?

## Chapter Six - Should We Tell Him He Has Autism/Is Autistic?

THIS IS A PERSONAL DECISION, and, as the legal guardian, it's up to the parents to decide.

Let's look at some of the pros and cons.

I often hear parents say that they do not want their child to feel different. They don't want him to think that he has a label. Their assumption is that if he has a label, he will feel different than all the other kids; he might feel that something is "wrong" with him.

The last one is important. I think the concept of autism being wrong or a problem is a notion that a child would pick up from the adults in his life. If you see autism as something that is less that all right, a not-all-right way of being, then yes, the child might pick up on your concern that there is something wrong with him if he has autism.

There are adults on the autism spectrum who would take great exception to this. And with good reason. But first, let's look at it from a parental point of view.

Before your child was born, you had expectations and hopes. You wanted him to be the perfect baby, have an idyllic childhood grow up to be a strong confident, successful, happy young person. Then, those niggly feelings came in, telling you that something might be different about your child. Whether the concern came from you or whether outside family members, friends or professionals first brought it up to you, it still is something to get your mind around. That perfect child that you had anticipated may not be perfect after all.

But who is? Not a single one of us is perfect. Actually, we might be a little annoying to be around if we were perfect. Everybody is different. And it's within those differences that autism falls.

AGAIN, from a parent point of view, you want life to be as easy as possible for your child. If your child has autism life is likely not going to be easy for him. It's tricky fitting into a neurotypical response when the world comes at you differently.

After getting a diagnosis of autism many parents go through something that is similar to a period of mourning. Hopes and dreams that you have had for your child are not going to look the way you had expected. That's your problem, not your child's problem; please don't try to make it to his.

You might shift your expectations or shift how you thought things might look. This is the same child you had before you knew about the diagnosis. You just know more now about how that child tracks and manages the world.

There is another concern for parents. Well, there is more than one but we will look at this one first. As a parent, you might have high expectations for your child and that is a good thing. Some parents who that if the child knows he has a diagnosis, he will use that as an excuse for bad behaviour or not trying. He might say I can't do that because I have autism. "I don't have to do that if I don't like it, as I have autism and it is not within my area of special interest". Yes, I have actually heard those words used by some kids and by their parents. Do you think that that is the way life is going to work for your child?

In my role as consultant, I have often had parents ask if I would explain to their child that he or she is autistic. Although I think ideally this would best coming from the parent, each family has a unique situation and makes their own choices. Whenever I have told a kid that he has autism never once have I had that child cry, get angry, defensive or deny the possibility. Odds are that your child will already feel different than his peers. He's noticed that he doesn't respond to things in the same way as others. Things that seem to come naturally to other kids may puzzle him. Without knowing why they are different, sadly many kids interpret this to mean that they are, in their words, "stupid".

Adults who have autism, especially those were not diagnosed until later in life, say they wish they had known when they were younger. It would've explained lots of things. My son can get a rant going about this. He thinks it's mean and unfair of parents to withhold that knowledge from their child. He says that if you don't know what it is then how do you know to figure out what strategies might work for you? There are similar sentiments expressed in the book *Freaks, Geeks and Asperger Syndrome*[1], (a book I highly recommend). In this book teenager Luke Jackson talks about his feelings about having Asperger Syndrome (a form of autism). I love his attitude. He knows he's different, and that's okay. He talks about things that are challenging for him and what works for him.

If you're still wondering if you should tell your child about his autism diagnosis have an online chat with those articulate adults who have autism and who will share with you some of their experiences and insights. There is a community of such people on Twitter; you'll find them if you use hashtag #actually autistic. Another good place to seek answers is the Facebook group Autism Inclusivity[2].

WHEN TO TELL your child is a good question. This is all subjective. In my personal opinion I would suggest you think about this when your child is perhaps nine years old, although I know 5-year-olds who have a good grasp of autism, learned from their parents. You don't need to give huge explanations about it being a neurobiological disorder, going into a lot of detail about neurology, but just talking about the differences might do for now. This might change depending on your child's maturity, level of language and intellectual functioning.

It's helpful for a child to understand about his or her possible sensory symptoms. I'll talk more about sensory issues in later chapters.

Another area for your child to start to gain an understanding is in the social world. It is likely he has already noticed that socially he struggles with some of the things that the other kids seem to have picked up on already. Simple things like how to join or be part of a group, to use give-and- take in conversation, how to talk with someone rather than *at* someone.

There is an excellent series of books and workbooks by author Michelle Garcia Winner called *Superflex*[3]. It will help you work with your child on some of the social thinking that is so important in being able to manage in group situations. As much as your child might enjoy solitary pursuits, life is still a group affair and we need to know how to manage being with other people.

At a younger age your child is likely still noticing that he or she differs a little from his peers. This might be a good time to talk about differences, how everyone is different. Some people have brown hair, some are blondes, some people have blue eyes, and some have eyes that are hazel. Some kids love playing Lego while others might be outside climbing a tree. Some absolutely adore Thomas the Tank videos where another child abhors anything to do with them. We all like different things. Talking about such differences is helpful with siblings as well.

MARY NEWPORT IS a woman with a diagnosis of Asperger's Syndrome. She and her Asperger's husband Jerry were featured in the Hollywood movie, *Mozart and the Whale*[4]. Mary says, "By first grade, I'd begun to realize that I'd become my family's most annoying problem." Imagine feeling that way as a small child.

You see, even at such a young age, Mary knew she was different. She felt different and she reacted differently than did others around her. Sure, she didn't know the diagnosis, but she was sensitive enough and intelligent enough to feel that difference and how others were responding to her. By telling her about autism or Asperger's, Mary would have had a reason for those difference, a "why".

A few years ago, some parents asked if I would tell their ten year old son that he was autistic. He listened carefully to my explanation then came out with this. "I always knew I was different. Now I have a name for it and know that there are others like me.

Cool. Thanks." He smiled and walked away. We talked a lot more over the next month and every time he had a new question or insight. He was calmer, less angry. And, he was more open to learning strategies that might help him.

# PERSON WITH AUTISM OR AUTISTIC PERSON?

How should you describe him - as a person with autism or an autistic person? This is quite a controversial question with feelings split strongly into two camps.

First, let's look at the "person-first" viewpoint. It began in the 1970s with the disability rights movements. This view espouses that the individual is a person first and autism is just a part of what makes him who he is, just as is having blond hair or being left-handed. He's a child first like any other child but with the add-on of autism.

This person-first language is used by most professionals - therapists, educators, etc. They want people to see the child first as an individual, rather than focusing on the label. They mean this kindly and it's a reaction to the time decades and decades ago where we lumped kids together according to their labels. Nowadays we would not describe someone as a "cerebral palsy child" but "a child with cerebral palsy", with a visual impairment, etc.

By focusing on the person rather than the disability, the hope is to reduce assumptions, generalizations and stereotypes. Often when parents receive the diagnosis about their child's autism the news will be couched in person-first language. Most professionals practising today will have been trained in this language. Here is a handout[1] on this put out by the US Centers for Disease Control on using person-first language. This link[2] will take you to an explanation on the benefits of using person-first language and a series of articles demonstrating this point of view. There is merit in paying attention to what the individual says. Here is a short video collection of young people who prefer person-first language[3].

In contrast, there are many autistic people who adamantly support the use of identity-first language. They say that they are autistic. To them, autism is not an add-on, but an integral part of their neurology. The "with autism" implies that it's something extra or even bad. They claim their identity firmly. The movement for identity-first is so strong that those not using it on some social media sites will get called out.

This is worth thinking about. To get some perspective, here are a few sites to check out on this important debate:

- Identity-First Autistic: Effecting Social Change Through Language[4]
- Autistic Self-Advocacy Network[5]
- 8 Reasons Why You Should Re-Think Person-First Language[6]
- "Autistic Person" or "Person with Autism" - Is There a Right Way to Identify People?[7]
- A survey asking disabled people which language they preferred[8]
- Neurodivergent Rebel's video on the language debate[9]
- Autism *Actually* Speaking[10]

AS YOU CAN SEE, there are very strong beliefs on either side of this debate. Throughout this book I have used both.

When talking to someone who has an autism diagnosis, why not ask them which they prefer? And, if your child is old enough, give him or her choice.

# WILL HE GROW OUT OF IT?

The short answer is no. He won't grow out of it and there is no way to make it all go away. If your child has autism, he will always have autism.

But that does not mean that the way your child is right now is the way he will always be. Of course not - no one is. We all grow and change and acquire new skills. The rate at which we learn, and the depth of that knowledge will differ but everyone can and does learn. This most definitely includes your child. But, in the words of Temple Grandin, "Once autistic, always autistic."

Is that a bad thing? Some, especially some autistic adults would say certainly not. They like themselves. They may view and interact with their world in ways that differ from that of neurotypical people, but different does not mean bad or wrong. It's just, well different.

We all know that being different can be hard. Not following the norm can be rough. True. Must it be that way? Perhaps we can play a part in making neurodiversity mainstream and acceptable. Maybe it is not the autism that makes it difficult for some to navigate this world, but rather how the rest of us respond to that person.

In the neurotypical world there is the assumption that we all like roughly the same things. The noise and the lights, smells and crowds are just part of life that we pay little attention to. Most of us are able to block out those extraneous things to get done what we need to do. But what if your senses were acutely aware of sounds, smells, lights, colors, pressure, etc.? What if a trip to the mall felt like torture, leaving you drained for hours afterward? That how it feels for many autistic people.

Have you heard about quiet shopping? Some stores are becoming more aware of the sensory challenges that may affect some customers so are holding quiet hours for these shoppers and their families. During these times, the lights might be dimmer, the music is turned off, there will be no loud announcements, and similar things. Sometimes these quiet shopping times are outside of regular store hours so there will be fewer people around. Small changes like this can make the world a more welcoming place for those with autism. And, autistic individuals are not the only ones with sensory sensitivities. They are common with sensory processing disorders, fetal alcohol syndromes and many other conditions.

BACK TO OUR ORIGINAL QUESTION. No, your child will not outgrow autism, but he will learn and mature. The autism he displays at age 4 may look very different than at age 14 or 24 or 40. But, it will not go away.

Would the world be as it is without the contributions autistic individuals have made? Maybe not. Referring again to Temple Grandin, she suggests that neurotypical cavemen would have been sitting around the campfire socializing while the autistic types went off and invented new ways of doing things.

There is no "cure" for autism but there are ways to assist the child in navigating his way in the world.

Read what these autistic adults say about Things We Love about Being Autistic[1].

# WHAT IS IT WITH THIS SENSORY STUFF?

So, what's up with the sensory stuff you keep hearing so much about? Well, actually lots. In fact, sensory issues might just be behind many of the behaviours that you're seeing that aren't helping your child (or you).

Sensory issues in autistic people are not straightforward things. You can be either under responsive or over responsive to sensory input. Even more confusing, these do not remain the same. Under certain circumstance you can be more sensitive than you might at other times. And if you are in an environment where many things are coming at you, all the sensations could pile up on top of one another and make something that you could normally tolerate feel almost unbearable, culminating in a meltdown.

You might've heard the term meltdowns. A

meltdown is different than a tantrum. All kids can throw a tantrum. A tantrum is when you are showing your displeasure about something that is happening or about not getting something you want. Tantrums require an audience and if the audience goes away the tantrum subsides.

A meltdown is something different. A meltdown is not a child trying to get their own way or control their world. A meltdown is when that child has reached their limit; they cannot handle any more and are totally overwhelmed and then it all spills out. The way it spills out doesn't make your child feel good and it won't make you feel good either. So, it helps when we can avoid or at least reduce the kinds of situations that will lead to a meltdown. No one wants to feel overwhelmed.

Autistic kids spend much of their life in a heightened state of arousal. That is exhausting both for them and for the adults in their life.

We will address the sensory areas one at a time in the next chapters and in no particular order because there is no hierarchy of sensory needs for every autistic person. You can't assume that for the majority of autistic people tactile will be an area that is highly sensitive for them. It varies individual to individual can change over time, even within a day, depending on what else is going on.

Ideally, when your child's body is receiving the level of stimulation that it requires, he will feel calmer and more in control. Here[1] is a sample sensory diet form you can use as well as a list of sensory activities that might help your child's body to feel more regulated.

After reading the following chapters on various sensory aspects you may want to learn more about how they might affect your child. While an occupational therapist trained in sensory matters would be the expert, I would recommend you talk to, while you wait for an appointment here are some free, online questionnaires that might give you a place to start:

- Sensory Learning Profile[2]
- Sensory process assessment for adults[3]
- Sensory process assessment for kids[4]
- Winnie Dunn's Sensory Profile Caregiver Questionnaire[5]
- Variety of resources[6]

## TACTILE SENSE

Tactile has to do with the sense of touch. This really has two parts to it – one is feeling things with your hand such as fidgeting with something and the other is how something feels on your skin. (The two are quite related though).

Sometimes people comment that an autistic child's behaviour changes with the weather. Possibly there is something to the theories about barometric pressure affecting people, but it could be something else. Some of you will live in temperate climates where the weather doesn't change much throughout the year but for many people there is quite a difference in temperature between summer and winter and, consequently, the clothing that we must wear.

Think about summer. For many that's a

time when we wear shorts, sandals and short-sleeved T-shirts. There are large areas of our skin unencumbered, where nothing rubs. Then comes fall and often the start of school. That child who has been used to bare arms all summer, with the feel of the sun and the wind on them is now being forced to put on long sleeves and long pants. Jeans can feel heavy and scratchy and rub in not good ways. Those sweatshirts we put on kids are often loose and sloppy which makes them brush against your arms and your torso.

On the heels of fall comes winter when we might need to bundle up even more. It might mean putting on this piece of cloth that weighs heavy on your head, feels tight and constricting and pushes your hair against your ear and on your forehead. Suddenly people are trying to make you wear mittens or gloves - scratchy things on your hands, making it hard to pick up things. Where your feet felt free and comfortable in sandals in the summer now, you're having to wear heavy, clunky boots.

The same difficulties can arise when the season starts warming up. Finally, that child has gotten used to the heavy, bulky clothing he or she was forced to wear all winter. Then comes spring and people are asking that child to remove the weight and the bulk that they have gotten used to. One little boy he told me that when people wanted him to take off his winter boots he feared he was going to float away outside because he was so light.

Think about that child who has become used to having his arms and legs covered then you expect him to go outside in short sleeves. There's the feel of the wind on his arms, the sun on his skin.

Now, we can't all live in areas where the temperature hardly varies all year. We live where we live. And kids can get used to these changes but when they exhibit behaviours during seasonal changes, we'll need to keep in mind what might be behind these things and do what we can to assist them.

That can mean helping them to find fabrics that are less irritating to them. For some it might mean cutting the tags off, so nothing is rubbing on the back of your neck or there is no seam across the whole of your sock driving the child crazy. For others it might mean gradually introducing the upcoming change.

SOME KIDS actually pay attention better when they are fidgeting with something. Think about adult behaviour. Do you know anyone who flicks the end of their ballpoint pen when they're concentrating? Do you know anyone who doodles during meetings? Taps their spoon? Raps her fingers on the table? Many of us do these things and they might be unconscious habits that we've developed in childhood that actually help us be calm or to concentrate.

Decades and decades ago in schools we wanted kids to sit at their desk with their hands nicely folded on the desktop or in their lap. Those days are long gone (and actually I'm not sure that they ever worked for many children). There are kids who are distracted by having something in their hand so you don't want them to have a fidget, but other kids actually pay attention to the teacher better when they are fidgeting with something in their hand. These are kids who crave tactile stimulation. Their body is under-responsive meaning that it requires a lot of tactile input for the sensations to register and they need a lot of this tactile input across the day. So, fidgeting with something can be a positive thing.

When I say fidget, I mean something that they can play with or move around in their hands. I do not necessarily mean their most favourite toy in the world because that could be too distracting and take their mind off the task that they should be completing. Stores sell stress balls for adults and if the person has a large enough hand, they can be a good thing. For many kids though these stress balls are too large for them to wrap their fingers around and get a good squeeze, so you might need to make your own.

An easy and inexpensive thing to do is to go to a dollar store and buy some balloons. Make them the helium quality balloons which are a little stronger. You might even want to place one balloon inside another just for extra strength. Fill that balloon with something like flour or cornstarch have the child hold it in the palm of his hand and fill it up just enough so that the child's fingers can squeeze around it comfortably. Then knot the end - actually double knotting would be safer.

Dollar stores are great sources for other fidgets as well. There are balls, there are squishy fidgets, different plastics, different textures and things like that. They will definitely get grubby over time and need to be washed or even replaced but you're only spending a dollar or two each time so it's not a huge deal.

Another thing to consider from a dollar store is a spool of ribbon. Depending on the child, various sorts of ribbon might appeal to them. You can find ribbon that is smooth and satiny, some that is velvety, some that has more of a texture like corduroy. Each spool is generally only a couple dollars. Cut off about 4 inches of ribbon at a time and give it to the child to rub between his fingers and play with. If it's an older kid who doesn't want anyone to know that they are fidgeting with something it can be stuck in his pocket and the rest of the class need never know. Yes, the ribbon is going to get very grubby, probably pretty quickly, but just throw it out and cut off another 4 inches.

I once knew a boy who had intense tactile cravings. It took quite some time to find out what worked well for him. What we finally settled on had absolutely no appeal to me but really worked for him. It was one of those plastic scrubbing things that you would use when you're doing dishes. When it was cut in four it was about the right size for his hand. If this grade four boy fidgeted with his piece of scrubber, he could easily get 20 minutes of solid seat work completed independently and accurately. Without that scrubby fidget he would not get five minutes done and even then, would require some adult assistance to do it.

WHEN UPSET, we might try to soothe a child with a gentle touch. We feel hurt when that child pulls away from our efforts to comfort him. That tiny wisp of caress on his skin might be akin to nails on a blackboard to a child who is easily over-aroused by tactile sensations. For that child, a firm touch might be far more appealing.

## AUDITORY

*I* once knew a seven-year-old girl who had an autism diagnosis and didn't show a lot of challenging behaviours. But at school as one winter arrived she seemed to change. This once quiet child began pushing and fighting with other kids and tantrumming. She would fight about putting on her winter clothing and going outside for recess. This was quite different than her previous behaviours.

It took a while of observing to try to figure out what was happening. When she was thrust into her snow pants you could see her face change as she walked down the hall, looking ready to blow. There was this swish, swish, swish of the legs of her snow pants rubbing together. We tried having her go out for recess without those snow pants and there was far less hassle. The sound was bothering this little girl. I realize that there are millions of kids who have swishy snow pants on in the cold winter and are just fine, but for this one particular child either the pitch or something about that sound just drove her. Her grandma sewed her new snow pants. These were made out of corduroy instead of that water-resistant material and didn't make the same sound at all. When she was given those, the behaviours, including the fighting and the tantrums, stopped.

What was bothering her was auditory input. Something about the pitch or the quality of the sound of those swishing snow pants really irritated her. Think about sounds that might bother you as an adult. A common one is nails on a blackboard. For me if I listen to music and there is something slightly off key, that really grates on my nerves. Some of us might relish going to a rock concert while others absolutely abhor the volume of sound that would onslaught their ears.

THERE ARE autistic kids who have incredible hearing. Parents say that they might be talking quietly in another room and their child can hear every word that is said. Teachers say they might be whispering to someone across the classroom and that one student can still hear them.

School classrooms nowadays are not quiet places. That is just the way it is. No longer are kids expected to sit silently throughout the day, but they are encouraged to discuss approaches and problems with one another. They are free to get up out of their seats, sharpen a pencil, get a book, ask the teacher question. There is movement and there is noise.

A few decades ago, many schools had hallways and classrooms that were carpeted. Then there were concerns about mould and allergies and many buildings removed all the carpeting. While possibly easier to clean, the floors that are left are definitely noisier than those classrooms where carpeted flooring absorbed some of the sounds. To a sensitive child this can be overwhelming.

Let's think outside of the classroom as well. There is frequent movement in the hallways outside of the classroom door, whether that door is open or closed. Many schools have metal lockers, and those lockers clang loudly as the doors are opened and closed.

Most schools have some kind of bell or buzzer that signals class change time, when it's time for recess or lunch or to go home, and those bells or buzzers can be at a frequency or pitch that some kids find difficult to handle. (Actually, I know some teachers who complain a lot about the type of bell their school uses).

Then, one of the worst sounds is that of the fire alarm. Schools are required to have fire drills and for very good reasons. In most places by law some of those fire drills must be a surprise, not planned. That might mean that only the administrator knows when the alarm is going blare for a drill and neither the teachers nor the students is aware. Safety wise, this can certainly make sense so that the kids have practised over and over what to do and how to vacate the building safely and where to go while you wait outside. But that sudden hugely loud noise can be really difficult for some kids who have auditory sensitivities. This includes many kids who are autistic, but many other kids might also be sensitive to the sounds.

The fire alarm simply has to be loud; there's no way around that. Some schools handle this by breaking the element of surprise. For just the one or two students who might be thrown into a total panic by the unexpected alarm these kids might be pre-warned. I know of one child who, even when he knew the alarm was going to ring later that morning, was in an absolute frenzy of anxiety before it happened then had a huge meltdown when it finally sounded. (In fact, his entire morning was a disaster as he anticipated this upcoming, terrifying noise). The principal made a different plan for the next surprise fire drill. He talked to the child ahead a time and asked for his help. He asked the child if he would please push the buzzer for him when it was time for the next drill. They spent lots of time talking about the purpose of fire drills and how to keep everyone safe and that this was going to be this child's job to help out the school. They drew pictures about it and went over and over a story they made up about fire drills. When the day came the child spent some time with the principal in the office ahead of time, then he donned his noise cancelling headphones and with his hand on the principal's, together they pushed the buzzer. Possibly since it was under his control and there had been so much planning ahead of time, there was no meltdown this time.

So, noise cancelling headphones can be a boon for anyone who has auditory sensitivities. We are not going to make our classrooms silent places; it's just not going to happen. For some kids, noise cancelling headphones can help them concentrate much better and to be calmer. Some kids who also have tactile sensitivities might not like the feeling of that headphone strap across the top of their head. For those kids they might want to wear that strap part against the back of their neck or down under their chin.

You can now get noise cancelling earbuds that will be far less conspicuous than headphones. Some kids keep them in their pocket and just pull them out when they need to quiet things down so that they can work better. Some don't need noise cancelling earbuds, just regular earbuds that will dampen down the sound a little bit. For some people, listening to music while they work is helpful and not distracting.

If you go to a pharmacy or drugstore there are lots of different kinds of earplugs you can find. The ones that I like are shaped almost like little foam drums that you can squish in your ear. They definitely do not remove all sounds from the environment, and you can often hear some speech sounds but it is muted enough that it could help some kids from becoming overwhelmed.

IN SOME CLASSROOMS you might notice a teacher wearing a head set, lapel or other type of microphone. This is likely connected to a sound field system. There are many brands, but they serve similar functions. They raise the sound of the teacher's voice above that of the hubbub in the room. That doesn't mean that the teacher's voice is necessarily louder, but it is more obvious, making it easier to pay attention to the teacher's words. His or her voice is carried wirelessly to a central speaker. Some are mounted permanently in the ceiling of the classroom; some are portable and can be carried from room to room. Many are also connected to Smart Boards so that videos, etc. can be played through the speakers. There are personal systems where the teacher's voice is projected to a device that a specific student carries, such as a child with a hearing impairment. My preference is for classroom-wide projection as it benefits so many kids.

Initially, some teachers will be reluctant to use the system and wear a microphone. They are self-conscious about their voice. They worry about remembering to turn it off when they leave the classroom. If they speak to someone in the hall, the staff room or use the washroom, all those sounds will be carried back to the classroom's speakers.

I have never met a teacher who did not cherish their speaker system by the end of the year, even if they were reluctant users initially. They say that they are less fatigued at the end of the day because they did not have to work at projecting their voice. Most report that kids pay better attention. And, most telling is the fact that when a substitute teacher is in the room for the day, the children remind the sub to wear the microphone because they prefer it.

Some lucky schools have a sound field system built into every classroom. More often though, one is ordered with the needs of a particular student in mind. At the end of the year, a built-in system must be taken out and re-installed in that child's next classroom. Teachers are sorry to see them go. While the teachers appreciate them, they are also helpful for kids who have hearing impairments, attentional issues, autism, fetal alcohol syndrome, and those with many other learning differences.

I'VE TALKED about the sound environment in schools because school is often a stressful place for autistic kids, but let's move on to our home environments now. There are noises in our living spaces that you are likely not fond of, but don't really think about because they are part of life. Take for instance the vacuum cleaner. It's probably only the rare person who truly enjoys vacuuming but we do it anyway. Think about the sounds - the running motor, the sucking noise, the clatter as bits of dirt move around the brushes and get gobbled up. The decibel level and pitch vary machine to machine, but some might be in that truly irritating range for a particular autistic child.

You're not going to abandon vacuuming, but keep in mind that the sound might contribute to your child's distress. Perhaps don't run the blender right before or after vacuuming if that high-pitched whirl bothers your kid.

I know a child who found it difficult to eat at the table with this family because the sounds of their chewing drove him up the wall. He described them as gooey, smacking, watery sounds and if he looked toward their mouths, he was grossed out by glimpses he could see of masticated food. His preference was to eat alone in his room; his parents wanted him to be with the family at the dinner table. The compromise was that he wore ear buds during supper. (Over time his auditory sensitivities decreased, and he was able to eat with others without covering his ears).

One form of auditory input that many parents hate is that of the automatic hand dryers found in many public restrooms. Some parents say that it's so hard to take their autistic child shopping or to a restaurant because they are terrified of the hand dryer sound. (What is worse - you and the child wiping your wet hands on your clothes or forcing him to use the hand dryer?) Hand sanitizer and wet wipes might become your friend.

IN A COUPLE of chapters we're going to look at proprioception. Giving your child proprioceptive input is often a good way to make auditory sensitivities easier to handle. It's certainly worth a try.

## OLFACTORY SENSE

Olfactory has to do with your sense of smell. Many kids who are on the autism spectrum are highly sensitive to smells. As a teacher or as a parent I would simply not wear perfume or aftershave. I don't think it's worth it. While you might enjoy your smell, it might be enough that it totally puts the child off their day.

Some kids can be sensitive to the odor left behind by cleaning products, including surface disinfectants and laundry products. While the television advertisements might extol the virtues of leaving behind scents on your clean laundry, that could be exactly what you do not want to do for an autistic child who has olfactory sensitivities. Some smells in a small amount might be very pleasant but if you ramp that odor up by ten or 20 times that's how it might feel to a highly sensitive child.

As I said before, with any of these sensory areas you can be over sensitive or under sensitive. If you are over sensitive, then even a small amount of input registers on your system. If you are under sensitive than your body requires a lot more input before it can register.

If the child is under sensitive in, say, the olfactory area, then they would be described as sensory-seeking. That means that their body is craving some of the stimulation to fill that void. The variety and intensity of smells might be just fine for you but to that child, who needs more before the sensation registers, there is an absence and he is seeking stronger smells. You might see such a child sniffing marking pens, or even worse, there are things that are more inappropriate for him to smell.

I know a young guy who really sought out strong odors. He would try to put his nose into the armpits of people, both people he knew and strangers. If someone got up from a chair, he would go put his nose where the person had been sitting. He would also put his nose to people's rear ends. As you can imagine, this was going to get him in lots of trouble, especially when he did it to strangers on the street.

Surprise, surprise, telling him "No" didn't work. Neither did "Stop that". And his parents tried giving him some negative consequences which didn't work either. What did help though was addressing his sensory need - that craving for more olfactory input. For one boy who was having this challenge he went with his mom to the store and they tried out all kinds of plug-in air fresheners till they found the one that he liked the best. That was on in his room nonstop. It solved the problem of trying to smell inappropriate things in public, but he then was spending most of his time alone in his room. So, the family found a plug-in air freshener of the same scent that was movement-activated and plugged it in the family room. Initially this boy walked by it what felt like 100 times a day, but he was getting some of the input he needed.

Another boy I know who was showing similar behaviours required even more olfactory input. He also liked to draw. His family found some marking pens[55] at an office supply store and these marking pens each had a very distinctive odor - awful odors to the perception of many people, but he loved them. (They include dill pickle, barnyard smells, etc. You can an example here[1]).

He also used nasal inhalers; one that he really liked was a lavender smell. You can get them in a variety of odors now and this child kept one in his pocket and used it quite frequently during the day. The upside was that he no longer tried to put his nose in people's butts or their armpits.

VISUAL SENSE

As you likely already divined, the visual sense has to do with the information that you take in with your eyes. Like the other senses, an individual can require more than average input to register or can be sensitive to even small bits of incoming information. And this level of sensitivity can vary for that person.

Years ago teachers of young children were taught to make their classrooms bright and colorful. Attention-grabbing objects would dangle from the ceiling and the room would be awash with bulletin boards, posters and artwork.

The trend in more recent years is to tone this down. It's not only autistic kids who can be over-stimulated and have their attention taken off-course by too much competing stimuli. Many of today's classrooms will have fairly plain walls where the instructor teaches. This means that the children's attention is focused on the speaker or the information that the teacher is portraying on the black board, white board or projector. There might be other very colorful areas of the classroom, but those are spots where the children would be directed for a specific purpose or for those kids who learn best with more intense visual stimulation. You will notice classrooms whose bookshelves are hidden by plain curtains that are only drawn back when the kids are invited to go to those areas. This is part of the term Universal Design for Learning. If you'd like to learn more about UDL, check out this link[1].

Cluttered classrooms can be disorienting to kids who have visual sensitivities. Their eyes might not know where to light and the mass of visual detail coming in could be overwhelming.

Some autistic people are excellent at details, but this can mean that they can't see the forest for the trees. The individual features jump out at them and demand their attention. They find it hard to let all that extraneous detail recede into the background.

This has to do with a term called Central Coherence. With good Central Coherence you automatically know which things in the environment you need to pay attention to.

With poorer Central Coherence, everything comes at you with the same intensity. It can take a lot of conscious effort to recognize and catalog all that input and purposely decide to let some things slide off while you focus on other aspects. For most of us this is a totally unconscious act. Imagine the energy it would take to have to concentrate on this all the time. No wonder autistic kids are drained at the end of a school day.

AS MENTIONED in the auditory chapter, our classrooms today are busy places with lots of sound and motion. Even if the noises do not bother a child, the motion might. A child who can ignore auditory distractions might be interrupted by the flash of color as someone walks by their desk.

Some classrooms are lucky enough to have individual study carrels available, a desk with elevated sides along 3 edges. This helps block out some of the visual stimuli in the room. But they are scarce in schools and there are certainly not enough for all the students who would benefit.

It's possible to make improvised study carrels but cutting a cardboard box so that it has 3 sides, without a top or bottom. Try for a box that is relatively the same size as a child's desk. When the box is not in use, it can be folded flat and lain along a wall. When a child feels that closing off his view of the classroom would help him work better, he could retrieve a box and spread it on his desk.

I am not a fan of having a strategy available to just one child. Why make him feel different? And, there are many undiagnosed kids in a classroom who would also benefit from certain strategies. If half a dozen such boxes are available for whomever would like to use one that period, why not applaud any child who understands enough about his own learning style to know what this technique would help him?

TO MANY OF US, lighting does not matter much. Sure, if it's too dark then we turn on a light to see better. But if you are sensitive to lights, then there can be a great difference.

Fluorescent lights flicker. Most people do not notice but someone sensitive would. (These lights also hum, potentially bothering a person who has auditory sensitivities). My preference would be to have no fluorescent lights in the building but that is not reality. Sometimes ensuring that the ballast is not wearing out will reduce that distracting flicker. But other accommodations might be needed. Some people find that wearing a visor or ball cap deflects some of the flickering from their vision and they are then less distracted. For some, sunglasses might help.

SLEEP PROBLEMS ARE NOT uncommon for autistic kids. Think about your child's bedroom. Is it a bright, highly stimulating place or are there muted colors, low lights and an atmosphere conducive to sleeping?

Tents can be wonderful things. They are cozy and feel safe, plus they are a nice way to block out excess stimulation. Have you seen child's bed tents? If your child has trouble sleeping, crawling into a tent on their bed might help.

And speaking of sleep, were you aware of the warnings about blue light impeding sleep? Blue light is given off by screens. Modern technology has made screen use so easy and so appealing. Even very young children know how to push and swipe and press with their fingers to make a device do what they want it to do. While once televisions were considered babysitters, smart phones, tablets and similar devices are now right up there alongside TVs.

I am NOT anti-technology and rather like techie things myself. I get that when parents come home from work and are trying to prepare supper, having a child amuse himself with a tablet is handy. The American Academy of Pediatrics has a statement recommending limits of screen time for kids[2].

Apart from the amount of time a child stares at a screen, there is also concern about *when* that child has screen time. Blue light surpasses the body's production of melatonin, a naturally occurring substance that helps us fall asleep. An hour or two before bedtime, restrict screen time. Instead let this be a time for a calming bath, having a snack, reading a story and snuggling. Read about How Blue Light Affects Kids and Sleep[3].

# GUSTATORY SENSE

*G*ustatory is all about our oral motor area, the mouth. It refers to things around the outside of the mouth, feelings on the inside of the mouth as well as taste. Let's start with the outside first.

Despite the fact that most of us learn to have some control over our drool by the time we reach our third birthday, some autistic kids have weak oral motor control and are slower in coming to this. Having saliva dribble from their lips may still be a problem when they are school age. A speech/language pathologist or/and an occupational therapist might be able to give your child exercises to help firm up his muscular control around his mouth to reduce the drooling. Even simple activities such as sipping through a straw can help develop the musculature in the oral region.

If a child is drooling, you might think that you should approach him or her when you see that saliva edging out of the corner of the mouth and down the person's chin, and gently mop it up very lightly and tenderly. But, this could have the opposite effect to what you are going for. Your tender ministrations might arouse feelings in him that you did not anticipate. The area around the outside of the mouth and particularly the chin and lower jaw can be sensitive areas for many autistic people and that very light caress on the chin could send willies down the spine of that individual. You know, that nails on the blackboard kind of shudder-inducing feeling. This could cause the person to freeze, to pull away, to be suspicious of the next moves that you might make or even to lash out or try to run away. Rather than that soft, almost-not-there touch swipe his whole chin slowly but firmly if that child has tactile sensitivities, particularly around his mouth. And, it wouldn't hurt to let him know ahead of time what you are going to do and why you are wiping up that drool.

A DENTIST MIGHT LOOK aghast at the shape of a child's teeth. He might turn to the parent and admonish them on the importance of daily brushing and flossing their child's teeth or the ramifications down the road will not be pretty. While the parent might look guilty and concerned, most likely it's not that they don't know this information. They are most definitely aware of how important it is to look after a child's teeth, but this may be easier said than done.

Let's look at some of the reasons why. The mouth can be a sensitive area, particularly for some autistic children. Often parents of toddlers begin dental care by putting their finger in the child's mouth and brushing the teeth that way, perhaps with some kind of cover over their finger. Or they use a washcloth. As the child's mouth gets a bit bigger, they may progress to using a baby-sized toothbrush.

Is brushing with a cloth or a wet brush enough? Generally, the advice is to use toothpaste. But let's hold off awhile before simply putting something into the child's mouth.

For a child with lots of oral sensitivities having something stuck into his mouth can be an unpleasant experience. There are even some toddlers who find the progression from breast-feeding or bottle feeding to having a spoon or fork in their mouth can be unpleasant. The metallic taste of a spoon can be abhorrent to some so the parents might use plastic. As the parent attempts to insert a toothbrush and rub it around those fledgling teeth the child might be actively squirming, trying to pull their head out of the parent's reach and their tongue will be trying to evict that intruder. Some parents get their fingers bitten while they attempt oral hygiene on their child. Having something placed inside their mouth can be almost repulsive to some kids.

Then there is the whole toothpaste issue. You will come across parents who have a problem with their child eating the toothpaste. Some of those pastes are particularly flavoured to appeal to children, including bubble-gum lovers. While those strong tastes might appeal to some children, this can be a real issue for autistic kids. Many find strong tastes abhorrent.

You might say that there are many, many toothpastes on the market and surely, the parent can find one that will appeal to their child. That's a logical assumption, but in my experience it does not always hold true. After a certain age, parents might be able to apply the suck-it-up factor and insist that the child simply tolerate that taste for the minute it will take to get the teeth brushed. To most of us that doesn't seem like too much to ask. But, if you are autistic and all day long your body has been assaulted by sensory invasions and you're at the end of your rope and exhausted, having to go through this ritual before bed could just be altogether too much and the child will have a meltdown.

But put yourself in the shoes of that parent. Like the child, you are tired; it's been a long, hard day. You just want to get this child into bed and asleep so you can put your feet up and recharge your batteries before you need to go at it again the next day. Is it worth the fight to brush his teeth? Couldn't we let it go just this one night and we'll make sure to do it tomorrow night? I can see you nodding your head. Yes, it doesn't seem like the end of the world to skip brushing those teeth one evening, but it's a slippery slope from there.

Say your child has gotten by the horror of having an object in his mouth, and there is one particular kind of toothpaste that doesn't instantly bring on the child's gag reflex. But then as you start brushing the teeth, the toothpaste sort of fluffs up in his mouth. It doesn't remain in that thick cream form, but it alters in his mouth cavity. How would that feel? Yes, I know you feel it yourself several times each and every single day. But you don't have autism and sensory sensitivities.

A dentist once told me that if a child has a major aversion to all forms of toothpaste, then just brushing with water is better than nothing. He also had another suggestion.

Place some baking soda in the palm of your hand and dip the wet brush into the soda. Then use that to brush his teeth. Again, there's a strong taste involved in that as well as a texture of the gritty substance on the teeth and in the mouth.

The sense of taste can be so particular to some children who have autism that taste and certain textures in the mouth can bring out their gag reflex. There are parents I know for whom it is just the norm that when they brush their child's teeth they know the child will throw up.

Because of the issues around taste and texture many autistic kids are very picky eaters. Getting a well-balanced diet into the child can seem almost impossible. Still, having a child throw up their bedtime snack is disheartening.

Along with taste and texture issues in the mouth there is also the question of temperature. Some kids will only want items that are lukewarm in their mouth and cannot tolerate anything too warm/hot or too cold.

Mealtime is a very sensory event. There are the tastes, textures and temperatures of the foods that we just mentioned. But there is a visual appeal (or the opposite) to the foods on our plates also. There are typical children who do not like their foods to touch each other. Or, they don't want to eat anything green. For an autistic child, multiply this aversive exponentially.

Food smells. Most often we hope that it is a good aroma but certain smells might be off-putting to an autistic child, either during the cooking stage or when sitting in front of a plate.

Then there are the sounds involved at the dinner table. Although we attempt to never chew with our mouths open, people with sensitive hearing will pick up on those chewing and smacking sounds. Forks scrape against plates, cutlery clatters and chairs squeak. Would your child eat better while wearing headphones? That might be a better alternative to having him eat on his own.

We'll talk about this more in the vestibular chapter, but some kids have weak trunk muscles and holding themselves upright can be quite tiring. You might notice your child slumping across the table or putting his head onto the table while he eats. Consider how he is sitting and the chair he's on. Can his feet touch the floor? You feel unstable when they don't. Perhaps a stool would help. Experiment with different types of seating for him. We'll talk about this more in the next chapter.

All of these sensory issues can make eating

difficult for some autistic kids. Parents often worry that their child has an unbalanced diet, but despite their best efforts, the child self-restricts his eating to just a few foods. Why? Because of some of the sensory things we've talked about already, plus another reason. When you are always on high alert, ready to protect your body from external forces that can over-arouse it, you tend to shy away from new things, sticking to the tried and true.

If you are worried about your child's diet, a nutritionist, dietician or some speech/language pathologists might be of assistance. There is an excellent program, often delivered by a specially-trained speech/language therapist and/or an occupational therapist. It's called SOS Approach to Feeding[1].

# VESTIBULAR SYSTEM

The vestibular system[1] is located in our inner ear, on the temporal bone, near the ear's cochlea but is not part of our hearing system. It has to do with our sense of balance, movement and letting us know where our body is in space.

Have you ever been on one of those merry-go-round-type rides on the playground? You know, the platforms that you run and jump on and then it spins around while you hang onto some poles or handles? Most kids jump off of those feeling delightfully dizzy and stumble around the grass for a bit.

There are some children whose body craves vestibular stimulation who can go around and around, get off such a ride and walk perfectly fine. These are kids who have fairly intense vestibular needs.

Another sign that a child is seeking vestibular input is that he will love to rock or really enjoy swinging and those activities have a calming affect for him. For most people the best type of rocking is a forward and back motion rather than side to side, although there are individual differences. Think about when you were holding a baby in your arms. Our instinct is to rock that child in a direction from their head to their feet.

A CHILD with sensory processing difficulties can also have the opposite effect and be easily overstimulated in the vestibular area. This might be a child who has a poor sense of balance. He is unsteady on his feet. He might be the last one in his age group who learns how to hop one foot or to skip or to ride a bicycle. Some people with vestibular sensitivities are prone to motion sickness as well.

VESTIBULAR IS a good sense to stimulate in a classroom. There will be many students, not just those with autism but kids who have learning disabilities, fetal alcohol syndrome, and attentional issues who will benefit from the type of stimulation you receive through your vestibular system.

A simple way to supply some vestibular feedback to the child's body is with an assortment of seating possibilities. Search on your favorite online store for seating cushions. You will find round ones, square ones or wedges that you fill with air. The amount of air you use will depend on what feels good to that child. These cushions fit on the child's chair and allow him to wiggle as he sits. That wiggling provides vestibular stimulation.

If the school is lucky enough to have chairs that are not permanently attached to the desk, then there are far more options available. Sitting on the therapy ball is great for some kids because it allows them to bounce up and down, to wiggle back and forth or side to side, giving their body the stimulation, it is craving. For some kids these types of movements actually help them concentrate better on what the teacher is saying and on doing the work. Therapy balls come in the typical round shape you might be familiar with and some have little legs on them to keep the ball from rolling away. You can buy rings that the therapy ball rests in to help keep it in place plus you can even buy a floor ring with a seat back attached to give more support. Therapy balls also come shaped more like a peanut that you straddle and that is comfortable for some kids. I would not recommend a child sit on the therapy ball all day long, however, because it is tiring for the trunk and abdominal muscles. You don't want the child to start slumping.

This may sound odd, but there are one legged stools that some kids love. It's just how it sounds. There is one leg down the centre of the chair with a wooden seat or a padded seat. The child can rock back-and-forth on it. There are also two-legged stools they give a similar affect. Some of these one- and two-legged stools have the leg adjustable so it will suit various sizes of kids.

Another type of stool is often made of tough plastic, but the bottom is not flat, it's slightly rounded and in a mushroom-looking shape. The round bottom allows it to rock back-and-forth. One brand is called Hokki[2].

With any of these stools make sure that the child can touch the ground easily. If his knees are not bent at close to a 90° angle, then strain could be put on his lower back.

You can buy child-sized rocking chairs that have stoppers on the front and back legs so that a child cannot over rock and tumble himself and the chair over him. Any classroom I've seen that has such rocking chairs finds that they are in high demand.

As I have mentioned before, I am certainly

not a fan of such tools being available only to the autistic child in the classroom. I would rather see several sets of all of these tools available to any child.

Who said that we have to be sitting down to learn? I've been in some enlightened classrooms where along the walls is a ledge about elbow high for the kids in that room. Students are free to take their book to that ledge and stand while they do their work.

Some lucky classrooms have standing desks. A standing desk is exactly how it sounds. They often have adjustable legs so you can vary the height based on the size of the child. When the child bends his elbow at roughly a 90° angle he should be able to rest the side of his hand on the desktop if it is about the right height for him. Some of the standing desks have a wire between the front or back legs that you can put your foot on and wiggle your foot back-and-forth. This added motion can be helpful. Other kids might like to stand on one of those seating cushions that I mentioned earlier. That will allow them to wiggle around. Some of these cushions even have what feels like ball bearings inside them to give greater feedback to your body.

If I had a younger autistic child in my

house right now there are three things I would feel strongly that I needed to have. One is a swing, preferably one both inside and one outside. The vestibular motion of swinging can have a very calming effect.

The second thing I would have is a tent. Think of those rainy days of your own childhood when you would take a sheet and drape it over a table to make a tent for yourself. Didn't it feel great to be cocooned inside there? You can get small, child size tents, even pop-up types that you can put in a corner of a room if you don't want your dining room table festooned with bedsheets. When your child starts to feel overwhelmed, crawling inside a tent can block out some of that excess stimulation and help him to calm down. You could even get tents that fit over a child's bed and might help him feel cozier when he is sleeping.

The third thing I would have is a beanbag chair. That brings us to the next section, proprioception.

## PROPRIOCEPTION

Now we are going to talk about proprioception,[1] and this sense gives a big win for those of you who work or live with autistic kids.

Place the palms of your hands flat on a table in front of you, or if you're not at a table put them on your knees. Now lean forward so that you are pressing your weight into your palms. Think about how that feels. The reason you can feel that pressure is because of something called proprioceptors. Proprioceptors are nerve bundles in the large muscles of your body. They help register body motions and the feeling of weight or pressure. And this is good news.

The reason why it is good news is that proprioception, weight and/or pressure, are ways that you can combat the other senses when they are being overwhelmed or over-aroused. Weight and pressure may have a calming effect.

And, I say may have a calming effect because no one strategy will ever work for every single person. What I'm saying will apply to many people and is worth trying. How do you know if it will work? Well if the person is old enough, ask them. Or ask their parent or caregiver. Or, try it and see if it has a calming effect. The child's reactions will let you know.

On occasion, you might see a child wearing an unusual vest. They are sometimes made of what looks like padded neoprene or sometimes they are cloth with pockets in them and those pockets contain different size packages of weights. The latter is a weighted vest. Sometimes the weights are applied across the chest and upper back. More often, they are in pockets near the lower edge of the vest. The former vest I described is one example of a pressure vest. They can often be snugged up with Velcro or some other type of fastener so that the vest will hug the person closely, giving a feeling of pressure. Again, weight and pressure can have a calming effect.

Some other examples of weight that you might see are ankle or wrist weights that people might wear when they are exercising. Sometimes these weights are not strapped around the person's ankle or wrist but instead they might be draped over the shoulders, or draped across the lap

With younger children you might see them with a lap weight. It might be a rectangle or round piece of piece of cloth stuffed with some heavy weighted material that they put on their lap. Some of the purchased ones are in the shape of a turtle or some other stuffed animal. There are also weights and snakes that are kind of a long thick rope-type piece of fabric that is stuffed with weighted material and the child might have it draped across the back of their neck and down the chest or it might be across their thighs. These are all examples of weighted products that might help make a child feel calmer. Or an adult, for that matter.

If a small child is upset, we might gently rub their hand or their shoulder to help calm them. If you are thinking about the powers of proprioception as a calming strategy perhaps do not stroke that child's hand gently, especially if he has tactile sensitivities. That soft touch could be unpleasant and over-arousing, the opposite of your goal. Instead, firmly hold or press down with more force on their shoulders. You might want to refer back to the chapter where we talked about tactile sensitivities for more cautions about gently rubbing anyone before knowing that they would welcome such a touch.

HEAVY WORK ACTIVITIES provide a sense of pressure and engage the proprioceptors. Your house offers many opportunities to use those large muscle groups, from wall push-ups to wheel-barrow races to doing the vacuuming. Here are 50 heavy work activities for kids[2].

Pushing and pulling are good proprioceptive activities. TheraBand and TheraTubing are useful for this. You can find them at exercise fitness shops and online retailers. They come in different strengths (levels of resistance); generally the color designates the strength.

Is your child forever kicking the table or chair legs during dinner? If some of the seating cushions we mentioned in the vestibular chapter don't help, consider tying some TheraBand around the legs of his chair. He can press on the stretchy band with his feet, giving his body needed proprioceptive input and perhaps allowing you to have a more peaceful dinner.

When a child is in the throes of a meltdown after being overwhelmed, the odds are slim that you can get through to him to do some heavy work activities. That is the time to just wait. Let him know that you're there if he needs you but keep your talking to a minimum and give his body time to wind down. Instead, think of heavy work a preventative measure. A healthy dose of regular heavy work will help, as will doing such activities at those earliest signs that your child might be getting over-aroused.

While it is great if you can get to recognize those signs, it will be even better if your child can gradually come to recognize those signs and take action on his own. Isn't that your goal? After all, you cannot always be with your child and you want him to be able to develop the skills so that he can self-regulate.

In the previous chapter I mentioned three items I would have in my house - a tent, a swing and a bean bag chair. The latter provides the body with proprioceptive feedback, especially if a child sits in an adult-sized one. The chair will fold around him and accommodate his movements.

When your child is upset, have you ever noticed him try to crawl under the couch cushions? He is instinctively trying to give himself proprioceptive sensations. If he likes that feeling of pressure on him, then he might love a bean bag chair. It could be especially helpful if you couple that with a weighted blanket. Weighted blankets even bring comfort to people who don't have an autism diagnosis. If you try a weighted blanket your child will quickly let you know if it does not suit him. If not, don't push it. Weighted blankets are available at specialty shops, many online retailers or you can make your own. A quick search on Pinterest, You Tube, or a search engine will show you lots of ways you can sew one yourself. The same holds true for weighted vests and pressure vests. If you make or buy a weighted product, you might wonder how heavy it should be. That would depend on the size of the child. While it might be tempting to put a twenty-pound weight on a hyperactive five-year-old, restrain yourself. The rule of thumb generally is that the weight should be about 5 to 10% of the child's body weight. This is just a rough guess though, and you'll need to experiment. Some vests come with pockets able to hold an assortment of weights, so you have some options. Here is some information on weighted products [63]that might help.

A common question is how long a weighted vest or other product should be left on. I have found no definitive answer to this. Some specialists say that after twenty minutes or so the body becomes used to that degree of weight and it is no longer doing its job. Remove the vest for an hour, hour and a half then you could try it again.

There are kids who insist on having the

same blankets on their bed all year round. While that heavy quilt might keep him warm in winter, he sweats throughout the rest of the year, but won't remove that quilt. That child's body craves proprioceptive input and is comforted by the pressure.

Some parents feel that their child sleeps better under a weighted blanket. If that works for you, great. Some therapists have concerns about spending that much time under the weight. Occupational therapists are the specialists in this area and great to consult with

A word about weighted vests, and this is just a pet peeve of mine. Don't put something on the child that makes him look dorky. Little kids might not notice nor care. And some older kids might not notice either, but their peers will. You can purchase weighted vests that are stylish - often denim vests not unlike those that their peers might don. Some look like hoodies.

There are also pressure vests. While they have no weights, they will give the feeling of pressure which works well for some kids. Some of these pressure vests have an air nozzle allowing the child to increase or decrease the amount of air in the vest, altering the amount of pressure he feels. These are discrete and no one need know that he is not wearing an ordinary vest or hoodie.

If you're unsure about your child sleeping under a weighted blanket, consider pressure instead of weight for his bed. Although there are lots of options to purchase one, here are directions to make your own stretchy sensory sheets.[64] If you're traveling, these sheets take up far less room than would a weighted blanket.

When you look up instructions for making your own weighted blanket, vest, etc. you will find a variety of suggestions for stuffing material. I've seen metal ball bearings, plastic pellets, dried beans, rice, grains and such. Consider the possibility that your product might one day develop a hole. If there a danger that your child or someone else in your home might eat the bits that drop out? Do you want to be able to throw the whole thing in the washing machine or will you use a removable cover? What if the amount of weight you want to use changes? None of these considerations should keep you from trying weighted products, just think about your options.

Back in the 1940s and 50s fur coats were popular. Ever seen those big, heavy things? I once scoured every second-hand shop I could find to pick up these coats. They weigh a ton and many kids loved them. Sitting on a bean bag chair, a fur coat draped over them and a hand stroking the fur helped soothe many kids.

I know a boy who relished the feeling of pressure on his feet. He would tie his high-top sneakers tightly, saying that they made him feel good that way.

Spandex biker shorts and tank or t-shirts can also give the feeling of pressure. A tight tank top can help some kids tolerate the feel of a loose, floppy sweat shirt.

HERE IS the really neat thing about weight and pressure - it can help counteract the effect of the other senses when someone is getting overwhelmed. Wearing a weighted vest into a gymnasium may help some kids tolerate the noise of that large, echoey space. A compression garment giving the feeling of pressure can help some kids tolerate the sounds, smells and distractions of their environment. Unlike with weights, there is not the concern about how long a pressure garment can be worn.

Think about the times in your homes that are trying for your child. Is it hard on him when company comes over? When things are out of routine during the holidays when extended family share meals at your place? Would it help if your child had access to a weighted blanket and a quiet place to sit when he needed to regroup or calm down? Might he be able to stand the noise and confusion better if he wore some type of weighted or compression garment? Would it hurt to try?

At school, gyms are often the hardest place for kids who are autistic and have sensory sensitivities. One boy told me that he felt dizzy when he entered the gym - the ceiling seemed so high, like it went on forever and he could get lost or float away.

If the child has olfactory sensitivities, gymnasiums smell (especially after the high school boys' teams have been practicing in there). Visually, things are different in the gym. Apart from that high ceiling, the walls are farther apart, there are bright, colored lines drawn on the floor and the lighting might differ from that in the rest of the building.

For a child with auditory sensitivities, the gym can be a nightmare. Sounds echo. Squealing voices come from all around. There's the thunk of bouncing balls, the slap of ropes smacking the floor and all manner of noises, depending on the activities.

Often when a classroom of kids enters a gymnasium the instructions are to run laps. This is a good warm-up activity but consider it from a sensory view. Many autistic kids have difficulty with gross motor activities and may not be as coordinated as their peers as they run in circles around the room. If he has vestibular issues, his sense of balance may be weak. To counteract this he might spread his legs in a wider stance and hold his arms out to the side. As he moves he might pound his feet into the floor, trying to give himself proprioceptive feedback to help ground himself.

If he has tactile sensitivities, he'll worry that some other child might brush his arm as they run past. He might hug the wall, brushing the edges with his fingertips.

(Unfortunately, he might accidentally rip some of the posters dotting that wall, but that was not his intention.)

His visual sensitivities make all the colorful clothing race by him in a blur, making it difficult to pick out the individual children, in turn making it all that much harder to dodge them so that his arm won't get brushed.

While he is struggling with all this, many of his classmates are having a great time. Their high-pitched giggles fill the air. Their sneakers make sharp squeaking noises irregularly on the floor. There is the persistent slap, slap of their many feet.

Can't you just feel the pressure building inside this child? He's trying his best to hang on, but it's becoming all too much and then what does that teacher do? She blows this piercing whistle and it's all too much and the child has a meltdown.

He's sent out of the gym (thank goodness, he feels). The teachers say that the upset came out of the blue - no one was touching him and nothing happened. Well, from the outside, it might seem that way, but the assault on this child was tremendous. Sure, last week he tolerated it, but that was different. Today his family woke up late and had to scurry around to make it out of the house on time. He couldn't find his favorite shirt and the sock he put on had hole in it, making his big toe poke through and you know how much that bugs him. In the morning rush he forgot his homework on the kitchen table beside his bowl of dry cereal because they'd run out of milk.

Any one, two or even three of these things might have been tolerable on a good day but the tsunami of little things built and built until it was all too much to handle. No, the meltdown did not come out of nowhere.

I am in no way suggesting that autistic children should not take part in gym class. They certainly should. The exercise is great, and it is part of the curriculum, but they might require some accommodations and understanding.

Perhaps he could do an alternate warm-up

activity, one in a quiet corner of the room. Perhaps he could be in charge of lugging out the gym mats or the ball containers and set things up for the lesson. He could run a timer or counter, checking the number of laps the kids run. While the others do their warm-up run, this might be a good time for someone to go over a social story with your child, letting him know what will happen during gym period.

Think about pressure and weight. Would the gymnasium be more tolerable if he wore a weighted vest? A compression vest? Ankle weights under his pants where no one would see them? None of these are difficult accommodations to make and could make a big difference to your child.

**Anxiety**

ANXIETY SEEMS to plague many autistic people. In fact, anxiety seems on the rise in the general population.

For autistics, the anxiety might be exacerbated by a couple things - sensory challenges and social communication difficulties. If you are always on guard, trying to protect yourself from possible sensory onslaught, you would be anxious. Our lives are full of social situations. If you have the feeling that things in the social realm are going over your head, that you don't quite get what seems to come naturally to others, your anxiety could increase.

Proprioception techniques can be your friend. Keep in mind that weight and/or pressure can have a calming effect and use this in anxiety-producing situations.

# INTEROCEPTION

Interoception[1] is often the most difficult sense to understand. For most of us, interoceptive skills are things we have never thought about. Interoception has to do with the ability to read our body's internal states. Our bodies give us lots of signals - they tell us when we're hungry, thirsty, tired, cold or hot, need to void our bladder or bowels, when something hurts, etc.

Our bodies have sensors throughout them. These sensors gather information and send it to our brains to let us know about our physical state.

Some autistic kids are slow to take to toilet training. Weak interoception might have something to do with this - they have decreased ability to recognize the sensations that tell them when they need to go.

Parents sometimes talk about how tough

their autistic child is with a high pain tolerance. Maybe. But it might be that those sensations of discomfort don't easily penetrate the child's awareness or if they do, he is unable to pinpoint the general feeling of malaise he has.

SELF-REGULATION IS a collection of skills we badly want our autistic kids to acquire. But regulation your emotional state has a lot to do with interoception.

We want our kids to be able to calm themselves. But to calm yourself you need to be able to recognize that you are upset. We know we're upset because of various body feelings - our heart might be racing, our breathing might be quick and shallow, our palms might be sweaty, our shoulders hunched, and our fists clenched. That's a lot of body awareness requirements. Self-regulation might come slowly to some autistic kids, but their interoception skills can also be delayed.

Sensory issues affect many autistic children (and adults). We'd like our kids to be able to recognize when things are getting to them, when they are becoming over-aroused. Without adequate interoception, it is difficult to recognize the signs that tell us when we are entering into those states.

This does not mean that your autistic child will always struggle with interoception or at least to this degree. As he grows and matures, so will this sensory system and he'll become more adept at recognizing his bodily states.

In the meantime, you can help by reflecting back to him what you observe. He may not be aware that you can tell he is angry because of his clenched fists, raised shoulders, rapid, shallow breathing and his red face. Show him in the mirror what you see and describe how this differs from his resting state. Take pictures to show him how he appears at different times.

When he is calm, have him join you in front of a mirror. Practice trying to make irritated or mad faces. Match your body posture to those emotions. Together, lower your hunched shoulders. Un-fist your hands, shaking out the tension in your arms. Control your breathing with a steady breath in, hold it for a few seconds then release it through your mouth.

Many of the fitness step trackers also measure heart rate. This kind of feedback might help your child learn to recognize when he is over-aroused and signal him to practice some breathing exercises or relaxation techniques to lower his respiration and heartbeat back to a calmer level.

While some adults find Tai Chi relaxing, the pace frustrates others. It's the same with breathing exercises and you'll need to experiment to learn what works for your child. Here are a few places to start:

- Deep Breathing Exercises for Kids[2]
- 8 Fun Breathing Exercises for Kids[3]
- 3 Breathing Exercises to Calm Kids of All Ages[4]

Just like with the other sensory areas, it is possible for a child to be over-sensitive in the interoception area. The incoming information from his body might feel like too much. So, in order to avoid the unpleasant sensation of being hungry, a child might eat constantly so that he doesn't have to experience that pesky feeling.

Interoception is sometimes called the 8th sense. It is only more recently known, and you might have more difficulty finding information on it compared to the other senses. If you're interested in learning more about interoception, consider these sources:

- Autism and the One Big Thing No One is Talking about - Interoception[5]

- Interoception, Neuroscience and Behavior[6]
- How I Feel - Making Sense of Emotions Through Interoception[7]
- Interoception: The "Hidden Sense"[8].

## HOW DO I GET HIM TO SHOWER?

"How do I get him to shower?" The first answer that comes to my mind about your shower question is, "With great difficulty." But, I suspect you already know that. This is a common concern with adolescent and teens and not just with boys.

There are several things at play here. The first is sensory and the second is interoception. Interoception is not as well known; it is the ability to read your body's internal states and often in autism, it is slow to develop. This includes reading the signs that you are hungry, thirsty, tired, in pain, etc. When we're in need of a shower, most of us begin to feel uncomfortable. Even if we don't stink, our scalp becomes itchy as oils build up and we know that our skin will feel better after showering. But, if you are unable to register and decode these body signals, you won't realize that you are feeling badly and you'll feel better after bathing. And, even though his body odor might offend others, odds are your child does not smell it himself.

Another related issue is changing clothing. There's not much point bathing if you then put on the same shirt you've been wearing and sweating in for days. The rule is you change your underwear and socks daily - even if they look clean and are your most comfortable ones. Rules are rules and must be followed even when you don't like them or understand the reason why they're there. (That is a handy parenting trick to learn - "The rule is...".)

The bathroom is a nasty place for anyone with sensory sensitivities. Because of all the porcelain and tile, it tends to be a noisy, echoing space. Sound bounces off of the walls. For those with visual sensitivities, light also reflects. The bathroom is full of smells - cleanser, shampoo, soaps, lotions, etc. This room might already have negative connotations if brushing teeth was an issue earlier on (due to oral/motor sensitivities). Then there is the tactile sensation of water pounding down on your skin.

Most people on the autism spectrum are rule followers. Once the rule is ingrained, they tend to follow it. So, the rule is that you shower each morning. Or evening or alternate days or whatever is appropriate in your house. Mark it on a calendar and his daily/weekly schedule. It simply must be done before he gets to do the things that he enjoys.

Saying, "Go shower" might not be enough. I know of kids who come out of the bathroom with wet hair but when it dries, it's greasy. While they might have stood in the shower that does not mean that they washed themselves. Likely, they require more guidance. You could make a step-by-step list such as:

- PUT SHOWER CURTAIN in the tub (or whatever to keep the water from going on the floor)
- Turn on shower taps and adjust water to right temperature (remember with interoception problems he could easily make it too hot or too cold without realizing it)
- Take off your clothes and get in under the water spray so that you are all wet
- Pour a bit (you might need to be exact about how big a dab is) of shampoo on your hand then rub it all over your head (standing erect while tolerating the water plus keeping his eyes shut might tax his vestibular system so you might consider baby shampoo that won't sting his eyes)

- Rinse out the shampoo (adding conditioner to the mix might be a bit much)
- Take the soap and rub it in your underarms and groin area
- Rinse the soap off
- Turn off the water and get out of tub
- Use your towel to dry off
- Comb your hair

- Put on clean clothes.

THESE ARE JUST examples of what you might list. Laminate the page, or place it in a Ziploc bag and hang it from the shower head or on the wall. Show it to him and go over and over it. Be firm about the time.

The tricky thing is also that sensitivities don't remain constant - they can lessen or grow stronger, depending on the stressors in the person's life and the maturity of their nervous system. Here are a few things to try. Smells were a huge issue for our son. I'd take him to a drug store, and we'd stand there opening and smelling deodorants. Sometimes one smell would overwhelm him so much that he could not take any more and we'd need to go home and try again a different day. We finally narrowed it down to one brand that didn't bother him quite as much.

Thought the problem was solved until he started avoiding even it. Back to the store. I discover a deodorant stone. It came in a plastic case and is a whitish soft stone; you wet it and rub it on your underarm. It has no odor. I am sure it's not as effective as most commercial deodorants, but it seemed to work. Drug stores and health food stores carry it.

Just like with the deodorant, you may need to spend quite some time finding a soap and shampoo whose scent does not disagree with your son. Sometimes health food stores carry unscented types. Baby shampoo might have less chemical smells. Or, you might run across an aroma that appeals to him, such as fruity body soap. Some body washes can even double as shampoo.

IF YOU SEARCH ONLINE, you can find social stories about showering. These are just a few:
- Autism and Hygiene: Sensory Overload[73]
- Personal Hygiene[74]
- Personal Hygiene Social Story[75]
- How to Take a Shower [76]

Here's a word of caution. You might get the showering rule was firmly in place in your house. Phew! Then one day you all sleep in and are late. You know, one of those days where you need to just throw on clothes and run out the door? Well, that might not happen. What you might hear is, "I always shower in the morning. That's the rule." Well, you might be late that morning....

## HOW DO YOU WORK WITH YOUR SCHOOL?

*H*ow do you work with your school? The first thing that comes to mind is nicely. If you spend much time on the Internet, you will hear some horror stories about parents and teachers or schools being at odds. Yes that does happen. But it is not necessarily the norm. And, if you are just starting to work with the school, you don't want to begin in a confrontational manner. Don't go in assuming that you need to fight for everything.

Let's look at this a little more closely. The centre of your universe is your child of course. That is understandable. And you are concerned about your child, to the exclusion of all else. Rightly so, your child needs you to be his champion.

Now let's talk about the teacher. Most

people who enter the teaching profession do so because they want to make a difference. They feel that they have a calling to help shape young minds. And, they enjoy kids. While they are in college taking their teacher training, most of these students are bright eyed and bushy tailed, and can't wait to get out into the world when they can actually start their teaching profession.

When they get that first teaching job, they are still eager and still can't wait even though a large number of them will be nervous about this.

Sometimes the realities of the job are tough. You know that already; any of you who have held a job know that even though it might be a job you really like there are hard parts to it. It is no different with teaching. Sometimes what the teacher thinks, the teacher wants, and the teacher believes is best is not what the system provides him or her.

In jobs that you have held, there have likely been times when you had to toe the party line, whether or not you agreed, whether or not you felt that that was the correct way to go. It can be the same with teachers.

YOUR CHILD IS ENTERING KINDERGARTEN, his

first real experience with the public school system. Or even a private system. Having your child enter kindergarten is a scary time for any parent. This is even more so when your child has a special need like autism.

As the parent, you want this new adult in his life to appreciate your child, to see all his good parts, to love and protect him. Over the last four or five years, you've grown to know and understand your child's, shall we say, quirks. By now you can often predict how he might react in certain situations. You know how he will respond to certain sounds, smells, textures, and demands put on him. That is wonderful, and he is lucky to have someone like you.

But this new teacher is not forearmed with all this knowledge. That's where you come in.

Many kindergarten programs have an entrance protocol where they might gradually introduce new kindergarten children to the room and to the teacher. This is a great thing.

The only trouble is that the amount of introduction typical a child might experience is not the same as what a child with autism might require. Kids on the autism spectrum rarely respond well to change. Change can be scary for anyone, but if you have autism changes often are even harder.

Autistic kids have difficulty making sense

of the world at the best of times. When things are new, they don't know what to expect. They don't know what will be asked of them. They don't know what might happen and how they might need to respond.

So definitely, by all means, participate in the general kindergarten readiness programs. But it will help if you do quite a bit more before your child enters the school system.

I'VE MET parents who are reluctant to share with the school that their child has an autism diagnosis. Autism is a medical diagnosis and as such the diagnostic information is owned by the parents until that child reaches adulthood and the age of taking responsibility for himself. It is entirely your right if you do not wish to share that information with anyone.

Let's look at the pros and cons of this issue. Some people hope that if that capital "A" word is never mentioned that no one will notice there is a difference with their child. There is a chance that could be true, but from what you know of your child, do you really think no one will notice that there is something a little different about the way he responds to the world?

Sometimes when people don't know about the autism diagnosis, the way a child interacts with other kids and with his world can be viewed negatively. It can look like bad, chosen behavior. If the choice is between people thinking that my child was badly behaved or that he was behaving in unusual ways because he is autistic, I'd rather that "A" word any day.

Many school districts will not be able to supply extra assistance for your child if he does not have a diagnosis. Now, there are some autistic kids who make it through their entire school career without any extra assistance or accommodations. In my experience that has been the rare child.

If you listen to adult autistic people who describe their earlier experiences, some of them, no scratch that, many of them, say that having accommodations and teachers who knew and understood would've made a big difference to their school experiences, and their mental health. So, take these notions into consideration, please, when you are wondering if you should let the school know that your child has autism.

Another concern parents have is with the school system. Not infrequently, parents are reluctant to share with the school the knowledge that their child has received an autism diagnosis. They fear that it will make the teachers think differently about their child, alter their expectation, or not challenge him academically. I'm not saying that that has never happened. But, it shouldn't.

Some autistic kids are in mainstream education placements with their age peers, following regular curriculum. Some are in mainstream classrooms following individualized programs. Some are in more segregated classrooms working on either regular curricular goals or individualized programs; many kids have a combination of all of these.

There is no one right situation. For some a mainstreamed placement is ideal; for others they fare better in a smaller setting. No matter what the environment, it should provide challenging academics that are within that child's reach but enable him to grow and build on his prior knowledge and experience.

LET'S say you do decide to tell the school. You'll need to do some upfront preparation work. Make an appointment to visit the teacher. You don't want to take up two hours of her time, but 20 or 30 minutes is very reasonable. This is a time when you can explain what your child is like and what he likes.

It would help if you go into the meeting with something written down. Two things are particularly helpful. One will be a copy of his formal diagnosis. The school will almost surely need to have that on the record for when accommodations are requested.

The second thing to bring is far more personal. You want to tell the teacher about your child. On paper, you can put a picture of your child. Underneath that have his name his age, his birthday, your name, the adults in his life who could be contacted if needed, including your home, cell, and work numbers. Be sure to include some alternates just in case they try to get hold of you and you're not available. The school should have two at least, but even better, three people that they can contact if needed.

Underneath that write down some information on what your child likes. What he likes to do, what he likes to talk about, what he likes to eat, everything that you think teacher might find useful to know. (And believe me, teachers often want to know more about this than you might think).

In the next section, write something about your child's typical day when he's home. How does he spend his time? What does he enjoy doing?

Is there any relevant medical information that the teacher needs to know? Does your child take medication? Does he have a seizure disorder? Does he have diabetes or hypoglycaemia? If he takes medication and there is a requirement that it be given at school and you cannot be there to dispense it, most schools require a letter from your doctor specifying the type of medication, dosage and time of day it is required. Some schools might ask you to sign a waiver saying that you will not hold them responsible in case of an error in medication dispensing.

Apart from straight medical facts, are there any other things about your child physically that will affect how he manages in class? Does he seem to have little sense of pain, so that if he falls and hurts himself he might not necessarily complain and the adults might not know he is hurt? Has he had a history of ear infections without letting anybody know that his ear or his head was hurting? Kids who have frequent or chronic ear infections often have some limitations in their hearing at least during those times of the infections. That's information that would be very useful for the teacher to know.

Does your child's behaviour go haywire if he's not eating enough? Either sufficient quantity or certain types of foods or at a certain interval?

Many kids on the autism spectrum are very picky eaters. It isn't that the parent has not attempted to supply their child with a good and varied nutritional diet but many autistic kids self-select what they eat. Is your child limited in what he will eat? If the school provides the lunches and/or snacks the teacher might need to know what he will or will not, can or cannot eat. Sometimes schools can only do so much in this regard. In the classroom the teacher may have little to no control over the foods that are supplied. If that is the case, then as the parent you may want to supply your own snack for your child. This is especially true on special occasions where students might bring in treats to share with everyone in the classroom.

Does your child have allergies? Many kids on the autism spectrum have either food allergies or food sensitivities or respond to other allergens in the environment. This is information that the teacher should know. Also, if he does come into contact with an allergen, how does his body respond? Does the teacher need to take any action? Is he asthmatic and would need to have an inhaler?

SOME OF THESE are necessary things to share but are not too difficult. Now comes the tougher parts. These are not necessarily easy things to discuss with a stranger, but you have knowledge that if you share with the teacher might make life very much better for your child.

What sorts of things upset your child? How does he respond when he is upset? What do you do to help him calm down? If he gets really upset, how long does this last?

When upset, does he want to be near an adult? Is he better off left alone? Is there a favorite toy, an activity, etc. that will help him regain control of himself?

Does he get overwhelmed in new circumstances? Is being with lots of new people hard on him? What do you do in such a situation?

MOST SCHOOLS HAVE a formal process of planning for a student who has special needs. These plans will often list the child's current level of functioning, goals for the coming school year, strategies that will be used and who will implement these approaches. Often (and ideally) parents are involved in these planning meetings and need to sign off that they have been informed and involved. Depending on your country and region these go by different names such as IEPs (Individual Education Plan), PPPs (Personal Program

Plans), ILP (Individual Learning Plan), EHC (Education, Health and Care Plan), etc.

Kindergarten is mainly about two things language development and socialization. Any child can benefit from both of those things. But both areas are often weak for a kid on the autism spectrum.

How does he respond to other children? Is he at the stage of solitary play or does he parallel play and tolerate playing alongside another child? Does he interact with other children? Does he dislike them being in his space?

If he has a toy that he is enjoying, say some building blocks, will he share? What would he do if another child comes up to him and wants to play with him or with those blocks? This is a situation that will most likely happen in the classroom. It will help if the teacher has some idea of how your child will respond and how to help him handle these types of social interactions.

I think you're getting the idea of the sort of information it's good to share with the teacher ahead of time. Now, at the same time, you don't want to scare this teacher. You don't want to paint a picture that your child is extremely difficult for you to manage, let alone a strange person who might have two dozen other children in her care at the same time. There's a fine line between that and not being forthcoming.

So that's the initial meeting. There is other preparation work that you should consider doing.

Most kids on the autism spectrum take in information that they see far more easily than that which they hear. Visuals (pictures) can be really helpful. I would suggest that you make a picture collection.

That first time you visit the school and talk to the teacher take along a camera or your smart phone and take some pictures. Take a picture of the teacher, the door your child will use to enter the school, the hallway he will walk down to get to his room, his classroom door, where he will hang his coat and his book bag when he enters the classroom. (It's a nice idea if when you talk to the teacher you ask her to pick which cubicle or cubby or locker your child would use then put a sign with his name on it there so you can take a picture of the exact place that will be his). If there are desks, take a picture of the desk where he will sit, although most kindergartens don't have desks. They may have a series of tables and chairs.

Take pictures of the room. Take a picture of where the kids might sit for circle time, some of the play centres, or other areas that are delineated within that classroom. Take a picture of the bathroom that he will use. Walk outside and take some pictures of the playground area where kindergarten kids will play. If the little children are restricted to a certain area of the playground take pictures of where he can go and which of the climbing apparatus etc. that he will be able to use. (You can see this in action in my novel, *Autism Runs Away*[77]).

At home, if you can, print these pictures out and make them into a book. It need not be fancy. You can label the pictures then staple all the pages together. This is a book that you will go over and over with your child. It will help prepare him for what will happen at school. Some people like to put such pictures onto their iPad or some other tablet and make a scrolling story that you can go through that way.

PICTURES ARE WONDERFUL THINGS, but they don't quite take the place of the actual thing. Take your child to the school a number of times. It's preferable that initially he go when other kids are not in the building. If there's a quiet time when he could go and just meet the teacher on his own, that would help. She can say hello to him, and he will have some quiet time alone to explore the room and the school building, especially the rooms where he will need to travel between such as the gymnasium, library, music room, washroom, etc.

Take him outside to the playground. Walk him around the outside perimeter of where he can go. Show him how to play on the playground equipment. That might sound like a silly thing to say, but seriously, many autistic kids do not know how to use some of the playground equipment. You can spend the summer giving him some of those experiences.

YOUR CHILD IS the apple of your eye and at home the world revolves around him. That's not going to happen in school. He will be one of maybe a couple of dozen children in the room. Often there is one adult for all those kids. Sometimes there is an assistant or teacher aide or an educational associate in the room as well. Still, if your child is used to having one-on- one attention a lot of the time, then suddenly having a one-to-ten or even higher ratio can be a rude awakening.

I'm going to be generic here because many school systems vary in how they handle this. There are some systems where, if they are given advance notice, application can be made for extra assistance in the classroom. This might be a TA (teacher aide), EA (Educational Associate) or other adult in the room to help out. Sometimes that aide might be there for just parts of the day and the teacher would hopefully have a say in when she most needs that additional help.

Sometimes it takes a while for that application to go through and the extra assistance to materialize. Ideally, if you talk to the school in the spring before your child begins the following fall, things should be in place by when school starts. This is not always the case. In some places the policy is to see how the child manages. If he doesn't settle in and things are quite disruptive, then extra assistance might be provided. This can be a worrisome waiting time for a parent. This approach is not necessarily all bad. I have seen kids who have managed better than it was thought that they would be able to. But you never know.

It is rare that a teacher does not want and appreciate extra assistance in her classroom. Most of the time, you will find that the teacher is on your side if you are requesting that there be an aide to help with your child. But even if the teacher puts in her request, classroom teachers don't have very much power. They are not the ones holding the purse strings; they are not the ones who make the decision about where these extra people are placed. As a parent, if you are upset that there isn't enough accommodation or assistance being made for your son, don't rag on the teacher. Work with her as an ally; you are both on the same side, wanting the best for your child.

SYMPATHIZE with the teacher about all the kids and the variety of need she has in her room. You might say that you don't care about all the other need she has in her class, and I bet that is true. But the reason you should care is because of how that could impact your child. You want your child to have at least his fair share of attention, if not more. But the teacher is dealing with several dozen parents who all feel exactly the same way.

Let's think again about that bright-eyed, bushy-tailed, brand-new teacher who is fresh from college and eager to start teaching her first class. Most new teachers think that if they are hired to teach grade 5 or grade 10 or grade 1 that they will actually be teaching subject matter of that grade level. It comes as a rude shock to them when they discover that a goodly proportion of the kids in the room are not working at that academic level.

"Then what?" they ask. Well, that's where the skill of teaching comes in.

FOR MOST TEACHERS, it is important to be a good teacher. That is part of their self-concept. In teacher training they learn how to teach reading, how to teach math, all of those kinds of things. Unfortunately, most teacher education programs offer very little in the way of teaching kids who learn differently. And, that includes autistic kids. This is sad, but true.

So teachers enter a diverse classroom often unprepared for the variety and breadth of needs there are in that room. Some react by doubling down on their learning. They spend all their spare time trying to acquire the knowledge that would help them better teach these kids. That takes a *lot* of time. Particularly for teachers early in their career, who are already required to spend most evenings working on preparing lessons for the next day.

A teacher might hear from a variety of sources, such as parents, their school administration, special education teachers, etc. that they need to use certain strategies to teach special learners. They might be told that they need to do A, B and C for the child who has attentional deficits. They might be told to do D, E and F for the child who is affected by fetal alcohol syndrome. They may have to do G, H and I for the child who has an intellectual disability. And then a whole host of other strategies for the child who has autism. On top of students with these diagnosed conditions, there are all these other needs and differences that the teacher must somehow accommodate during the day. When she has 25 five-year- olds in her room, life is overwhelming as a teacher. Some teachers are just about ready to throw up their hands, saying I just can't do it. So, one more irate parent coming in to complain that they're not doing enough for their child can almost seem too much.

NOW IN NO way is this right. And, again, as the parent you don't care about all those other kids; you are concerned about your child and that is your priority. But the teacher has to answer to all these other kids and their families.

I have found that overwhelming the teacher by demanding she do a gazillion accommodations for a dozen different kids in the room is a recipe for disaster. It's not humanly possible to manage all those different programs and keep everything straight. Instead, it makes life easier if you can focus on certain strategies that will work for a variety of kids in the classroom. This makes it less overwhelming for the teacher and you get more compliance.

One of those strategies is the use of visuals. If a teacher is only going to implement one strategy, I highly recommend that the use of visuals will make a positive impact on the largest number of kids in the room ( especially including autistic students).

By visuals I mean things that will help reduce the amount of reliance there is on understanding spoken words. Most of these kids are able to hear, but processing the language or making sense of what they hear is another story. Visuals can take many forms. Those pictures that you took before school started are good example of one form of visual. A visual schedule is also very helpful. It can be on the wall, on each table, in each child's cubby and places like that. A visual schedule lets the kids know what is going to happen. The events are sequenced. Sometimes you will have a visual schedule depicting everything that's going to happen during that day, but for some young children that long, long, long strip of activities is too long; it can seem to loom on forever and be overwhelming. You might want to have a visual schedule that just shows what happens between when the kids arrive first thing in the morning and morning recess or morning recess to lunch time or some interval like that. When you have a visual schedule in the classroom, you'll be surprised at how much all of the kids come to rely on it and check out what is going to happen next. This is a step toward independence rather than having the students depend on the teacher telling them what comes next. (You can see examples of how visual schedules are used at home and at school in the novels *Autism Goes to School*[1] and *Autism Runs Away*[2]).

LET'S get back to that child of yours who will be soon entering school. Before school starts, you can help with the visual schedule. I don't mean you're going to do the teacher's work for her and create one, but what you can do is get your child used to using a visual schedule. Make one at home. Post it on the fridge or someplace that is easy to reference. Make a visual schedule of what will happen in your child's day. You might want to have one in the bathroom as an example. Pictures there would show what he does in the bathroom - he uses the toilet, he washes his hands, he washes his face, brushes his teeth, etc.

You could have one on the wall of his bedroom that would show the order in which you wish him to get dressed. At the top of the strip might be a picture of a child in his underwear, the next picture would show him putting his socks on, the next one his pants, etc. You could do this by taking actual pictures of your child at various stages of his dressing routine and tape them on the wall. Or, photographs of the clothing. Experiment with what has the most meaning for your child. You can have a visual schedule in the kitchen for what your child needs to do to get his breakfast. If he helps you with chores such as setting the table, you could have a piece of paper on the table that shows where he is to place a plate, a fork, spoon, a glass, etc. You get the idea. Getting your child used to a visual schedule will make his transition into the school that much smoother. All these little things add up and will make life easier for all concerned.

Here is a great inclusion webinar by Paula Kluth[79]. While it's meant for educators, it will give parents lots of insights as well. And this just might be something you want to share with your school.

## WILL HE EVER TALK?

Will he ever talk? This will be a worry high on the minds of many parents and rightfully so.

Will he ever talk? Good question. You might speak to all manner of professionals like speech language pathologists, psychologists, therapists and educators hoping for an answer. I'm very sorry but none of them can respond to that question definitively. They're not putting you off; no one knows, you see.

For sure, speaking is the easiest way we have of making our needs and wants known. To my way of thinking it is the ideal form of communication simply because it is quick and easy. Easy, for most people.

But it's not easy for all. If you think a child is not speaking as well as he should be by the toddler years, then please make an appointment with the speech language pathologist. I use the term speech/language pathologist because that is common in North America. (Throughout parts of the British Isles you will hear the term speech and language therapist, SALT). These links will help you find an SLP in the United States[1], in Canada[2] and in the UK[3].

First let me clarify that I am not a speech language pathologist. Much of what I am going to say in the next couple paragraphs is based on what I have learned from speech pathologists and what I have studied.

Having a delay or taking longer to acquire spoken language is not at all uncommon in autistic children. While many typically developing children are speaking in sentences or at least long phrases by their second birthday, that may not be true of kids who are on the autism spectrum. In fact, ages four or five are when some of these kids become more fluent in using oral language. There is no magic number for sure, but if a child is not speaking by about age 9 then the odds of him becoming easily verbal are lessened.

Back to your original question. If you are playing the odds then yes, there is quite a good chance that he will talk.

Rather than using the word talk, some professionals might talk to you about language and a language delay. This means that your child has not acquired spoken language in about the regular time. I'm sure you are very well aware that kids start speaking at different times. In the Endnotes section of this book you'll find a link[4] to a chart that describes how kids typically develop speech and language skills between birth and age five.

Since you'll likely be talking to speech/language pathologists and psychologists, let's look for just a minute at some of the terms they'll likely use. They'll speak of speech and language as two separate things.

Speech is how we say words and sounds. Speech has three main components - voice, fluency and articulation. Articulation is how we pronounce sounds in our language, using our lips, tongue and mouth. Fluency has to do with the rhythm of our speech. We all periodically pause as we talk and repeat sounds or words. Someone who does this a lot might be stuttering. We make sounds by air being pushed through our vocal cords - this is voice, along with the pitch or loudness of the sounds we make.

Language refers to the words that we use to share our thoughts and get what we want. There are kids who might have fine language ideas they want to communicate but speech difficulties could get in the way of how well the listener understands the message. Many young children make some articulation errors (saying "wabbit" for rabbit, for example). When there are only a few articulation errors or the errors are consistent, we can still make a good guess at what the child is trying to tell us. In this case his articulation difficulties aren't affecting his ability to communicate using spoken language.

But there are kids whose articulation is so disordered or their phonological processing errors are so extensive that it is hard for someone to make sense out of what they are saying.

Language is further broken down into two categories - expressive and receptive. Expressive language is when the person is trying to communicate something. Receptive language is receiving that message. A child can have difficulties in developing both expressive and receptive, but not necessarily in both. Just because a child has difficulty communicating does not mean that he has similar difficulties making sense of what he hears, and vice versa.

THERE IS ONE VERY, very crucial caveat here. Please, please, do not assume that because your child cannot speak that he does not understand what is said to and around him.

I'd be very happy if you would read that sentence again. Please - it is so very important.

One thing that I absolutely abhor is when I am in a school and hear a teacher talk about a child in front of that child. Or, in front of others. They seem to assume that because a child does not speak, that he is also unable to hear or understand. Not true. While there are kids who have both expressive and receptive language delays, you cannot ever assume that this is so.

There are horror stories from formerly nonverbal autistic adults who are either now verbal to some degree or who use typing or some type of communication device to let us know their thoughts. They say they heard and understood all the things people said about them when they were nonverbal children. They could not talk, so people assumed they could not understand. This was not the case at all.

Just think about that. Think about what these kids might've over heard people saying about them. Doesn't that just make you shiver?

Amanda Baggs[5] is one such adult. She was and still is nonverbal. Most of her life people have assumed that because she does not speak that she is intellectually disabled and that she didn't know what people were saying to and about her. She now communicates by typing and a computer program or app turns her typed words into speech. You can listen to her thoughts on being considered an "unperson" here[6].

I so do not want you to one day reflect back, appalled about the things your then nonverbal child might have overheard you say about him.

THINK about how a typical child acquires their language skills. That child first starts listening to sounds and then imitates the sounds and the mouth movements that you are making. Babies go through a babbling and cooing phase when they are little, playing with language and the sounds they hear around them. Then later, your child might be saying only a handful of recognizable words but when you talk to that child, if you give him a direction or instruction, his behaviour might show you that he understood what you said. Understanding language comes before the ability to produce spoken language. Can you see where I'm going with this? Again, never assume that just because a child is not speaking that he cannot understand what he hears around him.

HAVE you ever undertaken the daunting task of learning a new language? It's not easy. In those initial stages you first try to distinguish the sounds that you are hearing and the way those sounds connect. Once you have amassed a small vocabulary you might be able to recognize those words when you hear someone else saying them, even though you're not speaking them freely yourself. Again, listening comes before speaking. (It's similar to a baby going through the listening phase where they can understand more than they can say.)

People who have grandparents who speak

a different language often say that they can understand what grandma says even though they struggle to speak that language themselves. Understanding language comes before being able to produce language. I never want you to be one of those parents' years down the road, who shudders to think of what you might've said in front of their child, believing that the child could not understand. (Are you getting sick of me harping on this? Good. I hope it will stick in your mind and that you will ensure that no one around your child speaks in front of him, assuming that he cannot understand).

HERE IS ANOTHER ASSUMPTION. Sometimes we think that not being able to speak equates with low intelligence. It might, and there are definitely people with intellectual disabilities who are nonverbal. But please don't assume that, because your child cannot talk, he is unintelligent. Here are a few obviously bright people who were erroneously assumed, when young, to be intellectually disabled:

- again, Amanda Baggs[7]
- Carly Fleischmann[8]
- Ido[9]
- Tito[10].

There are definitely people that have both an autism diagnosis and a diagnosis of an intellectual disability. Years ago, it was thought that perhaps two thirds of everyone on the autism spectrum also had an intellectual disability. That is changed and the estimates are now closer to 50%. But that might well be way off. You see, our standardized IQ test is based heavily on spoken language ability; perhaps half of the subtests in an IQ test require the individual to speak their responses. If a child is nonverbal, they're going to be severely penalized on these measures. Apart from that, autistic people frequently do not score well on IQ tests for other reasons. They might make different connections to the test material then were assumed when the test was standardized. Due to executive functioning difficulties they may have trouble with the time limits imposed on some of the subtests. Weaknesses in auditory processing can also lead to delays in responding on the test.

Perhaps this is a good time to talk a bit about auditory processing. Auditory processing is different than the ability to hear. You could have auditory processing weaknesses but have no difficulty hearing. Auditory processing is more to do with making sense of what is coming into your ear. Although most of us take it for granted, processing information is a complex procedure.

You have to listen to the words someone is speaking. You have to be paying attention; your mind can't be focused on other things. This can be a problem for some autistic people as their mind might be attuned to internal subjects rather than what might be in someone else's mind that they are trying to communicate.

Once you do hear those words they go into your brain and you have to remember them long enough to make sense of them. This is easiest when the words you're hearing can relate to something else that you have previously experienced or learned or discussed. For most people this is almost an instantaneous process but for some people they can have auditory processing delays.

If this is your child, then one of the biggest gifts you can give him or her is time. When we ask a question, we often expect an immediate response. But some people require a longer processing time. When someone doesn't respond immediately, we sometimes make the assumption that they didn't hear. Then you repeat it. Or, you assume that maybe they didn't understand the way you phrased it and you rephrase it. Don't do this for someone who has an auditory processing delay. Their mind is busy working on what you originally said. Then, you interrupt them with something new and those processing wheels have to start turning all over again.

WHILE YOU WAIT, think about your body language. Do not cross your arms, tap your foot, roll your eyes, or show signs of impatience. Believe me that will not help. Just quietly wait. For many of us silence in a conversation feels uncomfortable. Get over it. You might need to wait 5 to 10 seconds or even more. Truly that can seem like a long time but if you just wait the person might well be able to come up with the response you were seeking. While it can seem like a long time to you the person struggling to process what you said won't notice the time because their brain is actively engaged in making sense of what they heard and formulating a response.

I mentioned that auditory processing is not the same thing as having hearing loss. But hearing loss is something we need to discuss.

WE'LL SPEND some time talking about hearing

because that is something that could affect your child's ability to acquire language.

If your child has a hearing disability his language skills will be seriously reduced. It does not hurt to have your child's hearing checked. This is particularly true in cases such as your child has a delay, a history of allergies or ear infections.

Think about sticking your head underwater in a swimming pool. You can still hear the sound of talking and yelling around or splashing in the water, but the sounds are sort of muted and distorted. If you're a small child with partially blocked hearing that's the way you hear sounds. If this continues for quite some time it will have an effect on your language skills and your language development. A small child learns at a rapid pace during those preschool years. If he misses even several months of hearing, that can affect his rate of learning.

Ear infections are common in childhood so what is the big deal? Well, it can be a big deal. If excess fluid or infection in the ear is blocking the free movement of the eardrum then the child will not be able to hear correctly. There hearing might not be totally blocked and frequently is not, but it could be impaired to some degree.

Think about that baby who was cooing and babbling, imitating the sounds that you are making. But if that infant has a hearing impairment, he won't be hearing those sounds or at least some of the sounds. If you can't hear you can't imitate and practice.

Some people talk about how quiet their child was. While that silence might give the parent some peace and quiet at times, it is concerning. What if that child can't hear? Or can't hear some of the time? Some children are prone to ear infections. Ear infections can crop up after they've had a cold or influenza etc. They can also occur often in kids who have allergies. Some babies get fussy or might rub their ear which gives you a clue that there might be possible ear infection. Other babies don't give those signs especially ones for whom this is the way they feel much of the time.

It is not always easy for any parent to know when their child has an ear infection. This might be especially true of kids who are on the autism spectrum due to interoception. We have a whole chapter on it elsewhere in this book, but just to give a quick explanation - interoception is the ability to read your body's internal signals.

Parents sometimes say that their autistic child has a really high pain threshold. Well, possibly, but it might mean that that child cannot differentiate where that uncomfortable feeling is coming from. It might take an intense sensation before it registers. Or, the child may have had that discomfort for such a long time that they're used to it; to them, that is just the way life is so why would they mention it to anyone?

Another factor here is Theory of Mind[11], another troublesome area for many autistic kids. Your child might assume that if something is in his mind, it is in yours as well, so there is no need to tell you. We also see this in toddlers - that child might want something but not have the words to tell you. They'll assume that you know and are purposely thwarting them from getting what they want as you madly rush around trying to offer what you think the child is after.

There are a number of reasons why you may not realize that your child has an infection. (Don't feel badly, it happens to us all). When a child's behavior seems to take a negative bent and you can't pinpoint the reason for the change, take the child to a medical practitioner to check for things such as a bladder infection, ear infection, etc. Or, consider that their mouth might hurt from a dental condition.

So, let's assume your child has had a series of ear infections and it's suggested that he has his hearing checked. Just because your child is autistic do not be leery of having his hearing assessed.

What will likely happen is an initial look at the child's ears from the outside and using an otoscope to see what it looks like. They might also check inside his mouth, the state of his tonsils and adenoids and possibly his sinuses as well to see if there are pockets of infection.

The actual hearing test will look differently depending on the audiologist that you're seeing and the set up used. Often you and your child will go into a sound booth. The child would have on headphones that will direct tones, noises and words into one or the other of his ears. Ideally what happens is that the child will give a signal letting people know in which ear and when he has heard a sound. Initial instructions might be for him to raise the hand on whichever side the sounds came in. Some audiologists are quite skilled at working with even very young children and devise ways to know when the child has heard something.

Because of difficulty your child might have in following the directions the results could be questionable, but they might give you an idea on whether it appears that your child is having hearing difficulties. There are different ranges and pitches in which we hear sounds; there's a certain band where we hear things called sibilant sounds - S, Z, and SH. It's not uncommon when a child has an ear infection, especially a chronic one, that he has reduced ability to hear these sibilant sounds. If a child can't hear those sounds, he cannot repeat them so a child with his hearing loss might say "oo" instead of shoe, it might just be "wing" instead of swing, etc. Other sounds that might be difficult for a child with a hearing loss to pick up could be th, v or f.

For some kids, antibiotics might be required. Some will have tubes inserted in their eardrum to help allow the fluid to drain out and relieve some of the pressure. Often this will improve the child's hearing.

Say you have had your child's hearing checked and as far as can be determined at the present time he does not have any hearing loss. So, you're not looking at hearing aids or any kind of assistive hearing device. Then the reason for the language delay is not due to her or his ability to hear.

So, what then, you ask?

This is harder to understand. We don't generally think about how a child acquires language; somehow, they just do. We did it ourselves and likely no one ever questioned how we were doing it. Those connections were just made in our brain, and gradually we could produce sounds to form the words and communicate our ideas.

Easy, right? Not for some. For a fair number of kids on the autism spectrum these connections are not easily made and speaking aloud their thoughts is not at all simple. But just because a child is not able to speak does not mean he is not thinking or that he is unable to understand what is said to and around him.

Are you still wondering if your child will acquire speech? Here's a study[12] on this question and it is encouraging.

Again, I am going to harp on this. Too many times to count I would be told by a parent that it doesn't matter if we talk about a child in front of him because he doesn't talk so he cannot understand us anyway. Statements like this make my heart fall to the floor thinking of just how often people have spoken about that kid in front of him. Please don't ever assume that a nonverbal child cannot understand what you are saying. Please be respectful.

## WHAT IF HE NEVER TALKS?

Do you want him to talk or to communicate?

"Well, of course I want him to talk and to communicate. They're the same thing," you say. Well, not quite.

Speaking is one way that we communicate but there are many other ways. Mothers and teachers are the masters at nonverbal expression. Think back to when you were in grade 5. Couldn't your teachers silence the class with just a look or body stance? Not a word needed to be spoken but the message was clearly communicated. (Parents gain skills at this when they're out in public with a misbehaving child).

Although we can communicate ideas and wants through our facial expressions and body language, speaking is a straightforward way to convey messages. For most of us, it's easy, requiring little conscious thought.

But for those who are nonverbal or minimally verbal (more on that in another chapter), this easy-speaking option is not open to them.

Being nonverbal is not the same as not having anything to say.

I would appreciate it if you would read that sentence over again please. I don't know who first said that, but it is powerful. Please go back and reread that line.

Think about why we speak. We want our needs and wants met. We want to share ideas and express pleasure.

Say you have a child who may understand everything that is said to him and everything going on around him, yet he is not able to form the words to tell you so. What you need to focus on then is a way for that child to communicate, to get his or her message across.

Can you imagine what it would be like to be unable to express your needs? Think about your child. Some of those unwanted behaviors might be just be due to frustrations in not being able to let you know what he wants or needs.

So, you ask, how can you help them to communicate? Well there are number of approaches from simple signing, picture cards to complex computer apps and programs. Especially for a young child or someone new to this system, consider a simple way to start and remember that this is a new skill you are teaching him.

Picture cards are one way to begin. Pick something that the child loves or often wants. Before giving it to him, show him the picture card of the object, pairing the picture with the actual object. Some of you with drawing skills might sketch the object. Those of us less talented might rely on ready-made line drawing cards. You can find a nice (free) beginning set of such cards here[1].

What do you do with these cards?

Is food a motivator for your child? Start with his favourite foods or snacks - maybe pictures of a glass of milk and a glass of juice. Show him the pictures and couple the picture with the actual object. Do not expect him to get the connection right away; you'll need to teach him through repeated pairings, explanations and letting him have his choice.

These pictures might be used in your daily routine. Paste a picture of the bathtub onto the bathtub and point the pairing out to your child until he makes a connection. Gradually, when your child wants a banana, he will be able to point to the picture of the banana, telling you that is what he wants instead of the picture of the orange you offered.

Giving a child choice is wonderful but making choices is a skill that needs to be taught. Allowing a child choice gives him power.

Some families display an array of pictures on the wall or fridge and the child can go pick one when he wants something or bring a picture to you to demonstrate what he wants. And especially while you're in the initial teaching phase of this if he brings you a picture of a glass of juice, give him juice.

Some people couple these sorts of pictures with a story. Carol Gray first started the term "social story". You can learn more about social stories at this link[2].

A social story is a way of letting a child know what's going to be happening. If you make a social story don't assume it's a one-shot thing. It's good to read them over and over with a child.

Some people shy away from social stories, saying they're not writers or they're not artists. Doesn't matter. Trust me. My stick figures can portray a social story that kids understand. I tell them what the figure represents, and they believe me, for some reason. You don't have to have your pictures, or your social story printed out in full color, laminated with borders, etc. Nope, just something drawn on a napkin in a restaurant can often work. Try it.

If you live in a techie household and gadgets abound, there are dozens and dozens of communication apps you can put on your tablet, your phone or your computer. Some are quite complex such as Proloquo2Go[3]. It is an absolutely excellent program but (and you knew there was about coming, didn't you?), it's very complexity can turn some people off in the initial stages. It is possible to use only simplified portions of the program if that's what suits your child's need, then as his skill level increases you can bring in more buttons and categories and choices. Again, this is a program that is wonderful but on the pricey side.

If you do a search on the Apple app Store or the Google app store for communication apps, you will find a big array of them. Some of them will allow you a free sample or a temporary download while you try it out. I would definitely advise this because there's such a difference in them and some just might suit you and your child more than others. Many of them are under $20.

The apps will do something similar to what I was telling you about with the picture cards. There might be a series of pictures under the heading Drinks so a child would look through and see a picture of a glass that symbolizes the drink he wants. He would then touch drink of his choice. In some programs he would show you his choice; others will speak that choice aloud, either as a single word or in a full sentence, including "please". You generally have a choice about the type of voice the program uses.

As the parent, you can control the number of these choices. For instance, in a household that does not buy soda pop, you'd delete or not have soda as one of the choices.

Of course, you would also keep the number of choices quite simple initially while the child is learning. Many of these programs are robust enough that you could continue using it for years and are appropriate for adults. I will list a few examples of these in the Endnotes. They are by no means endorsements nor am I favouring one over the other, but this is just to show you examples of what you might find out there[4]. (You will likely come across the term AAC when you're looking at apps. AAC stands for Augmentative and Alternate Communication).

There might be an advantage to having the same app on your tablet at home as you do on your phone so that if your child has gotten quite used to it and you are out someplace without his tablet, he could still use your phone.

Many parents are concerned about the amount of screen time their child has, and with very good reason. A concern about using an app on your tablet for communication is that that child could justifiably become glued to that tablet. It's one thing if a tablet is dedicated only for communication but it is another thing if that tablet is possessed tightly by a child who uses it mainly for gaming. I'm not saying that a child should never play games nor that she should not use a tablet, but this is a parental choice you need to keep in mind.

Those of you who might have backed away from using social stories due to concern over your story-telling or drawing ability are in luck in our technological age. There are a number of apps to help you out with social stories. We'll talk about just a few but search around; you'll find one you like.

Pictello[5] is a favorite of mine due to its ease of use for non-techie people. It's a visual way of creating social stories (and many autistic people are highly visual). Please take a look at it in action as a mom demonstrates how she and her daughter use it[6].

One question parents sometimes ask is if using some form of AAC will prevent their child from talking. The answer is a resounding NO! Think about it. If you are thirsty and want a glass of juice, what would take more time - saying, "juice, please" or grabbing your tablet, turning it on, calling up the app, swiping through until you found the icon for juice, pressing it and showing the tablet to your mom? In fact, often AAC acts as a bridge to the child developing speech. No, using AAC will NOT make your child lose his motivation to speak. You can read more about this here[7]. In fact, AAC can have positive effects[8] on speech and language development.

So AAC, whether a simple picture card, a robust app or a stand-alone communication device (such as Dynavox[9]) will not prevent your child from speaking. Of course, all these neat apps require power. Someone has to remember to recharge the device or keep spare batteries on hand.

Have you ever forgotten to charge your phone? You feel abandoned, don't you? But what if that device was your primary way to communicate with the world? The fall-out might not be pretty.

A LESS TECHIE option is sign language. A problem with using a tech gadget is that it runs out of juice. If your child uses sign language, he always has his fingers with him.

One thing that always bothers me is when a child learns sign language and uses it at school as his primary means of communication but no one in his house knows how to sign. To me, that seems so isolating. So, if you are going to use signing as a way for your child to communicate please, please make sure that everyone in the family learns how to sign as well.

There are a few different types of signing. Likely the most common is ASL American Sign Language[10]. Another one is Signed English. The difference between the two is that in Signed English every word is signed and that includes the ifs, ands, buts, etc. It follows the spoken or written English exactly. In ASL some words can be grouped together to form a concept and every single conjunction and word of the phrase might not be signed as well. Far more people understand ASL then do Signed English.

While ASL is fairly standard throughout North America, it differs somewhat from British Sign Language[11] although both use gestures, facial expressions and body language to communicate a message.

Makaton[12] is popular in the United Kingdom. It uses symbols and signs to support communication, following word order used in speech.

Sometimes kids who are autistic also have difficulties with fine motor coordination, or an additional diagnosis of Developmental Coordination Disorder, making it difficult for them to manipulate their fingers into the proper position for sign language. This can be frustrating for the learner and make it hard for the recipient to decipher what the signer tried to get across.

One solution to this might be baby signs; they usually require simpler finger movements and are designed to be manageable by very young children.

If you look online and do a search for baby sign[13] you will get lots of websites that show you simple basic signing. There is a lot of free information on the internet if you want to get started with baby signs[14]. Many parents use baby sign with their children to help their kids communicate before they become verbal. It can be quite effective, and those parents think that it reduces the child's frustration and tantrums because they have a way to get what they want. That power really means a lot.

ONE THING we have not talked about is

apraxia[15]. Some autistic kids also have a diagnosis of apraxia or childhood apraxia of speech. It's also known as developmental apraxia or verbal apraxia. (Non-autistic children can also have apraxia).

An apraxic child will have ideas in his mind that he wants to communicate, But the messages his brain sends to his muscles in the mouth region do not come across correctly. It's a problem of planning movement and carrying out movements. Apraxia ranges in severity. Here are some examples[16].

If your child is apraxic, will speech always be this hard for him? A qualified speech/language pathologist would be the best person to ask about your individual child. I can tell you, though, that of all the apraxic kids I have met, they have all been able to communicate through speech more easily over time and with therapy. This is something that an SLP can help with. You'll find more in the Endnotes at the back of the book on apraxia[17].

Let's circle back to how we started this chapter. What if he never talks? It might be best to have some nonverbal people share their thought on this with you. Remember, the goal of speech is communication. How well do the following nonverbal people communicate?

- Phillip - "I have nonverbal autism. Here's what I want you to know."[18]
- Ido - Ido is a nonverbal autistic man continuing his education in college[19].
- Kaylie Clinton - "Hear me speak without a voice."[20]
- James Potthast - nonverbal high school graduate writes a blog.[21]
- Emma - "I am an Autistic teenager whose body and mouth-words do not always pay attention to my bright and wise mind."[22]
- Noah - "Being nonverbal doesn't mean I can't think."[23]
- Mike Weinstein - once thought to be intellectually disabled.[24]
- Carly Fleischmann - nonverbal young woman who has a YouTube channel.[25]
- Amanda Baggs - "About being considered retarded".[26]

[2] SOCIAL STORIES HTTPS://CAROLGRAYSOCIALSTORIES.COM/SOCIAL-STORIES/WHAT-IS-IT/

[3] Proloquo2Go communication software app https://www.assistiveware.com/products/proloquo2go

[6] Watch a demo of Pictello https://www.youtube.com/watch?v=9B1fAaAS3N4&t=38s

# WHAT DOES MINIMALLY VERBAL MEAN?

For some of you this term will be new, but you will come across it from time to time. Depending on the individual it's referring to, it can mean two things.

Some kids are not totally nonverbal - they do have some spoken language. They might use just a few, single words such as hi, bye, please, thanks, no, mom, dad, dog, more, etc. For most neurotypical kids, this is the way talking begins, with just a few key words then their vocabulary expands from there.

Even if they begin speaking later than their same-age peers, these few words can also be the beginning of being able to use speech to communicate and their expressive language abilities will continue to broaden from there.

For other autistic kids, their language

might seem to get stuck at that stage, adding only some new words as the years go by. Often when a child begins to speak some words it's an encouraging step to more advanced vocabulary. But for some kids their language does not expand beyond a few words and phrases.

There are children with autism who do not tell their mom or dad when they want something, recite a story about their day nor respond when asked something. For much of the time they are nonverbal. Yet, that child might repeat word for word their favorite scene from a video. Or, rather than answering his dad's question, an autistic child might repeat the question.

Frustrating? Can be, but it might be a way for the child to process what he heard and come up with what he wants to say. It could be a way to stall while they formulate a response. Another child might take pleasure in the sounds of certain words or phrases and repeat them over and over. Perhaps they soothe him or are a way to practice.

Have you heard of the term echolalia? Immediate echolalia is repeating what was said immediately after hearing it. Delayed echolalia may involve repeating something heard some time ago. People are often amazed at the memory of some echolalic kids who can accurately recite whole streams of dialogue from movies or conversations they've overheard.

Some might describe echolalia as "non-functional language". Hmmm. I am not sure about the non-functional part. Sure, echolalia to us is not a swift way of getting our message across, but to the person using echolalia, it might well perform a function. Here are a couple excellent explanations of echolalia. If your child has echolalia, please listen to these short videos.

- Here's an autistic opinion on echolalia[1].
- Ask an autistic - what is echolalia[2].

YOU WILL ENCOUNTER autistic people who can carry on a nice conversation and tell you all manner of interesting things. From this you might assume that they are skilled in verbal communication. This may be true much of the time but under certain circumstances this ability may seem to become minimal or to desert them completely.

These circumstances often occur around times of anxiety, fatigue or sensory overload. When their system becomes so overwhelmed, they may lose the ability to speak.

"Why?" you ask. Again, hmmm. For most of us, this is hard to understand. Either you can talk, or you can't. But it's not that simple. Whether or not it's politically correct, you may have heard the term "struck mute", referring to when something happens, and a person is at a loss for words. It's sort of like that, which could happen to any of us. But within a few seconds our ability would kick in and we could speak a coherent thought.

For some autistic people, when this occurs, they may be minimally verbal, able to get out just a few words or phrases. Or they could become nonverbal. Even though lots of thoughts are swirling inside their head, they can't get those thoughts out in words.

Consider just how frustrating this must be. And how terrifying. People who have previously heard them speak will wonder what's going on. They may accuse the person of purposely refusing to speak.

Think about school situations. An autistic child has intentionally or inadvertently done something wrong and the teacher is asking him/her about it. This is a child who usually speaks. But when put on the spot, the child remains silent. Sometimes from his face you can see the internal struggle going on. That could be interpreted as a child trying to figure out how to get himself out of trouble or as a child who is unable to form the words to explain. One is a normal kid thing, the other isn't. Refusing to explain could be seen as an act of defiance, getting the child in even further trouble, when in reality the kid could be so anxious and upset that the words simply won't come. Do you think that raising your voice, stepping closer or threatening consequences will change the child's ability to explain? Likely any of these actions would ensure that the child will be unable to express to you his thoughts or feelings for an even longer period of time.

Aside from the social and embarrassment factors of minimally verbal or nonverbal situations, let's consider the safety aspects. What if an autistic person is accosted by the police and cannot respond to the officer's questions or even give their name? What if there's a medical situation and the person is so distraught that they cannot give pertinent details? This is a time when an augmentative or assistive communication system would be vital. Something as simple as a piece of paper would work. If you want to learn more about some of the different communication systems, refer to the chapter Will He Ever Talk.

## WHAT IF HE TALKS TOO MUCH?

*W*hile some parents would give anything to hear their child call their name or share a story with them, other parents would like a moment's respite from their child's constant talking.

This was often true of kids who had the diagnosis of Asperger's Syndrome. Asperger's was listed in the previous version of the DSM (Diagnostic and Statistical Manual of Mental Disorders), falling within the autism spectrum. Diagnostically it differed from autism in that the child did not have an intellectual disability and had no delay in acquiring spoken language. These children were sometimes referred to as "little professors" due to the way they would hold forth on topics that interested them.

With the revision of the DSM in 2013, the

variety of labels under the autism umbrella were removed, simplifying the diagnosis to just autism, but with levels one, two and three, which indicate the level of support that individual might require and the caveat of with/without intellectual disability and with/without language delay.

Even if the label has changed, you will still know autistic kids who talk a lot. Why do they do this?

We don't teach typical kids how to converse with others; they seem to pick such skills up on their own. There is reciprocity to our conversations - person A talks for a few sentences, then person B takes a turn as the verbal ball goes back and forth. This is part of the social communication that does not come naturally to autistic kids.

Part of social communication is reading the body language and facial expressions of those around us. Again, this is something we rarely teach neurotypical kids but these subtleties can be a mystery to autistic people. It's from reading these cues that we can sense when we have talked too much and and are boring the listener.

When our conversational partner looks away, averts their head, dips a shoulder down and away, shuffles their feet, etc., we realize that they are attempting to get away. At that point we can try to repair the conversation, to draw them in again by asking them a question, letting them have a turn to speak.

But if you don't have the skills to read these body signs, you would be apt to carry right on, especially when the topic is of great interest to you.

One of the diagnostic points for autism is "special interests". While most seven-year-olds know a lot about dinosaurs, an autistic child might have an encyclopedia's worth of knowledge on the topic. And be oh so willing to share that knowledge with you. These intense interests can be delightful and might lead into wonderful career possibilities down the road.

In the meantime though, constantly hearing about that subject can be hard for those around. While the topic fascinates the speaker, those around him might be far less enthused. Besides the feeling of being lectured at wears thin.

I knew an adolescent who knew everything there was to know (or it seemed that way) about real estate in his city. Every Sunday he and his dad toured all the open houses they could find. This child knew about the history of local land development, housing values, zoning, you name it about real estate. And, he was oh so willing to share this information. While to a certain degree it really was interesting, the kids on the playground did not enjoy standing around listening to his lectures on real estate every day. They would simply leave; the boy did not understand why they'd abandon him and did not want to learn about this fascinating topic that he loved so much. When this is just the neatest topic ever, why wouldn't you want to share the information with others? What he saw as enthusiastically sharing bored other people.

SOME PEOPLE PROCESS information better when they speak out loud. The act of hearing the words helps to imbed meaning for them. There is nothing wrong with that strategy in some situations but when in the company of other people it can cause problems.

Expressing thoughts aloud can interfere with the learning of others in a classroom or work situation. The noise might interrupt the concentration of those in the vicinity. When someone speaks our instinct is to pay attention to them, so ignoring them might be difficult.

During a test situation you can see how a child speaking out loud to himself could cause problems. Since it is a valid strategy and likely helpful to the child, that student might be better served by writing his exam in a quiet spot alone.

Subvocalizing is talking to yourself but at such a low volume that others may not be able to hear the words. Learning to subvocalize might help in situations where the person is not alone and free to talk aloud. Some kids learn to "talk in their head", still carrying on the dialogue but without speaking aloud. (Although better for those around them, it might not be as effective for the individual as it lacks the auditory feedback that might have assisted them).

Some autistic kids carry on a steady monologue while they play alone. Again, they might be using oral language to work through situations or practice skills and it is not only autistic children who do this.

EVEN IF YOUR child has not picked up conversational skills on his own, you can teach him. The Endnotes contain the following five resources that might help:

- Small Talk Can Loom Large: Teaching Your Child the Flow of Conversation[1]

- Six Tips for Teaching Conversation Skills with Visual Strategies[2]
- Teaching Conversation Skills[3]
- Teaching Conversational Skills[4]
- How to Teach Conversation Skills to Students with Autism[5]

## SHOULD WE MOVE TO FIND BETTER SERVICES?

*D*esperate, loving, well-meaning parents will do anything to help their child. Like other mammals, we humans are prone to believing that the grass will be greener on the other side of the fence. Often parents have asked if they should move to find better services for their child.

It's a personal decision that no one can make for you. But please don't make any hasty decisions.

Yes, you want the best for your child - that goes without saying. Of course you do. But what that "best" looks like is highly individual. If you think that there is a perfect therapy, therapist, school or setting for your child, I would caution that that is likely untrue. Yes, some will suit your child better than others and some will fit your family life and values better. But perfect - doubtful. And what is ideal for your child at age 4 might not at all be the best fit when he's 8 or 16.

How lucky your son is that the whole family is willing to give up everything and move for his sake. As to which locale would be ideal for your son, well that's a tough question.

I live in Canada and am more familiar with Canadian educational systems than those in the US. When I spent five days at the Autism Leadership Academy in Fort Lauderdale, I discovered that there are more similarities than differences in how we actually work with kids with autism spectrum disorders.

I would assume that at least in principle, the educational services available for your son should be the same no matter where in the US you live due to the federally legislated IDEA, etc. While on paper the services should be the same, I realize that the reality may differ.

It's a rare school district that does not have its special education (or SEN) policies posted online, along with contact information for whom you should talk to. Past the district level, states, provinces and counties will also list their initiatives and policies on their websites. Carefully check out the differences and talk to the people involved.

Apart from all this research, *why* exactly do you want to move? If you are seeking the ideal place in which to raise your son, I'd worry that it may not exist. I've talked with families who believe that if only they were in the right place, if only they had the correct teacher aide or special ed teacher, or program, then their child would be "fixed" or lead a more typical life.

Unfortunately, (or not!) while strategies can be learned and kids grow and mature, as Temple Grandin says, "Once autistic, always autistic." In fact, many articulate adults with autism take great exception to the idea of anyone trying to fix or change them. While they realize they may differ from the general population, they like who they are.

IT GOES without saying that your son's well-being is extremely important. But he is just one person in your family. What if you found what you felt were the ideal set of services for your boy but adequate employment was an issue for the wage earners in your family? Or you were torn between your duty to your child and your responsibility to ill, aging parents residing in another part of the country?

Young adults tend to have minds of their own. Even if you feel you've located your family in the perfect location for high school, post-secondary and work opportunities, your son may have different ideas. He may want to go to college elsewhere. He may seek job or school opportunities several hundred or thousand miles away. He may respect your opinions but still choose to move or make his own decision. (While worried, you'll be proud that you've raised a child who can think for himself and has the confidence and skills to strike out on his own.)

It's hard to judge a place by the services that are available, because even amid that array of services, many may be things your son does not need. It's hard to believe that there is that one correct way of working with every person with autism, just as there is no one correct way to teach reading. Each of us is unique. Even though he has autism, there aren't uniform traits across the spectrum, just tendencies that he may experience to varying degrees. And what your son experiences as a weakness at age eleven may differ from things that may cause him trouble when he is twenty.

Since the incidence of autism is so prevalent now, most schools have at least some experience with students with autism spectrum disorders. By contacting the State or Provincial Departments of Education, you will gain some idea of their policies regarding children with autism.

# HOW DO I GET OUR RELATIVES TO UNDERSTAND?

This is something you might not want to hear. There seems to be a "get it" factor with autism. Some people "get it" and some don't - they have a harder time getting on the wavelength of the autistic person and understanding what life might be like from his perspective. With time and assistance, some of your relatives will come to "get it" but some possibly never will. That's okay. You can live with that fact as long as you and your immediate family understand.

But you aren't always in your nuclear family - there are extended family celebrations and visits. This is when things can get a little trickier.

REMEMBER BACK to when you first suspected

that something might be different about your child? Those niggly little feelings when you would watch him do something or interact with his environment or other people?

Perhaps you shared some of your concerns with your best friend, the grandparents or other relatives. You might have received reassurances that you're just an over-anxious parent. You might have been told things like:

- It's just your imagination.
- You're looking for trouble.
- All kids develop at their own pace.
- Boys are quite different from girls.
- Just wait until he gets to school - things always straighten themselves out by then.
- If you ignore it, it'll go away.
- Aren't you being a little hard on him?
- You can't compare him to your brother's child who is a prodigy or genius.
- I have a friend whose second cousin's son was late speaking then talked a blue streak and was just fine.
- There is nothing wrong with that child. He's perfect in every way.
- He's bright and there's so much going on in his head that he doesn't have time for the things that interest other little kids.

Now, think back to when you learned the diagnosis. You might have been relieved to finally know. Or you might have regretted starting the investigation because now it is confirmed and there is no pretending that there is nothing different.

There can be a period that is almost akin to a type of mourning. We all have hopes and dreams prenatally about what our little bundle of joy will be like. He'll be the perfect baby, toddler and student, smart, capable, the kind of child other kids look up to and gravitate to. Or, not so much.

Those idyllic images pretty much never come to pass, not for anyone. But you love the child that you have.

But when your child has a diagnosis, you know that he is different. And, different often means that things will be harder for him. This is not something that any parent wishes for their offspring. The path less trodden can be challenging. Those challenges will certainly be felt by the child but also by the parents who are trying to support him.

All those things that you felt can affect his relatives as well.

OLDER PEOPLE especially might struggle to accept that your child has a diagnosis. You see, back when they were children, students who learned differently were shuttled off to separate schools and rarely seen again, or into a closed classroom within the building isolated from the general student body. Students who learned differently frequently simply left school because the type of help they needed was not provided, mainly because different learning styles were not understood back then. Disabilities were hidden away or spoken of in hushed tones. If they knew someone with a diagnosis back then and recall the way that person was treated, they would certainly not want that sort of treatment to happen to your child. Better pretend that it does not exist rather than run the risk of him being labeled and shunted off somewhere.

There was a time when labels precluded many things such as interacting with the general population. Back in the day, little was known about autism and the diagnosis was rare. The word autism might have brought up an image of someone sitting on the floor in a corner, rocking back and forth and banging his head. It's not that there aren't some autistic individuals who might do this some of the time, but certainly this is rare. It's only in recent decades that the "high functioning" end of the autism spectrum has been recognized. (Here, by "high functioning" I am meaning people who have intellectual ability within the average range or higher).

Apart from these older views, there are

other reasons why some relatives might have a hard time understanding your child's diagnosis and what it means in your lives. You might hear comments like:

- You baby him too much.
- Just throw him in with the other kids and he'll be just fine.
- All he needs is some discipline.
- He needs rules and expectations.

The latter statement I agree with and likely you do too. But what you think about discipline, rules and expectations might not be what your relative has in mind.

THERE ARE genetics involved in autism. If your child has a diagnosis, there is a chance that someone else in the family also has some signs of an autism spectrum disorder. Perhaps Uncle Harry recognizes some of his own quirks in your son (or Harry's wife has told him that she notices similarities). What if this hits too close to home and Harry does not want to think that he also might be different? After all, he has managed all these years; why should that not be the same for your child?

LET'S think about the requirements of family

get-togethers. They happen infrequently, so they cannot be counted on. While your child may have settled well into the pattern on which your household runs, these sporadic forays into extended family gatherings are harder to predict.

When you have difficulty making sense of the world, rules, routines and patterns are a source of comfort - something to rely on because you know what is coming next and what is expected of you.

Christmas is a biggie. We'll talk about holiday celebrations in the next chapter.

# HOW DO WE HANDLE CHRISTMAS AND HOLIDAY CELEBRATIONS?

Christmas. This supposedly joyous time can bring consternation.

Difficulties arise before Christmas Day is actually here. Whether or not your child actually enjoys school, the structure and routines are often a welcoming atmosphere for autistic kids. They know what's coming next. They've come to know what will be expected of them. They are familiar with the room and the people in it.

This lovely predictability in the classroom often disappears during the month of December. Even the vibe in the room can be different. Kids are getting excited about the possibility of what the Christmas holiday season might bring. Teachers often try to carry on and stick to the regular routine, but they, too, are tired. They have families and demands on their time outside of the school day. Christmas is supposed to be an enjoyable break; instead, it can be a time of frenzy and stress and too many obligations. So, the teacher might not be his or her most patient self.

Many schools hold some type of Christmas concert or celebration. This requires practice time and that practice time is carved out of the regular school day, so the typical classroom schedule can be thrown all out of whack. The autistic child is expecting to do math right after recess but instead the teacher calls them to go to the gymnasium to practice. That is not what is supposed to be on the schedule. The change itself can be disconcerting. Then, the practice time might not be with his own room with just his classmates but it might be combined with students from other classrooms as well. Again, it's not part of the usual routine.

Kids can be excited during the month of December. Sometimes, in an attempt to settle the kids down, the teacher might do something unexpected. When she knows that the children are getting too restless to do their normal seat work, she might decide to read them a story, have them sing songs, have them take an early recess even though that recess bell has not yet rung. For some kids these sudden switches might be welcome and help them settle down but for an autistic kid who relies on routine and knowing what is coming next these can be upsetting.

Again, whether or not your autistic child is enamored with school, he is used to it. Monday to Friday he is in school. But in December, holidays roll around and that child might have a week or even two weeks off of school, breaking his routine. These things are enough to throw a guy off his stride.

Now, think about things at home. You might run a tight ship in your household, with your home being neat and orderly. Everything has its place. But, suddenly there is this Christmas tree stuck in the house, in a spot where it just should not be. As pretty as it might be, again it's another disruption in the routine and change can be difficult for an autistic child to handle.

While those sparkly decorations and twinkling lights might enhance the atmosphere you're looking for, those flashes might not appeal to your child. They might catch his eye as light flashes, they might take his attention off what he was thinking about or trying to do. And all the while, in the back of his mind he's aware that that tree is suddenly glowing where it ought not to be. Sometimes we use a real Christmas tree rather than an artificial one. The smell of the Pine may evoke memories of Christmases past and can be a pleasant smell for many of us but if you have autism an unusual aroma might be bothersome.

AS THE CHRISTMAS SEASON APPROACHES, the child's parents might seem different. They might be in a flap, with shopping and wrapping presents and baking goodies. All this needs to be squeezed into an already busy day. There's also financial stress as sometimes we might get carried away and spend more than we had intended. All of this can make for harried parents who might show less than their usual amount of patience. Couple this with the child who is discombobulated by all the changes at school and now he's home and it's a Tuesday and he's not going to school; the combination can be volatile.

NOW, it's Christmas morning. Some kids are very early risers on their big day hoping to awaken and unwrap their presents. That disturbance to the usual rising hour can be just one more thing that seems difficult to cope with for an autistic child. Getting kids to sleep on Christmas Eve when they're excited and anticipating what gifts they might receive can be tricky as well. Many autistic kids have sleep issues where it's either difficult for them to fall asleep or to stay asleep. So with that early morning rising, the child might be even more sleep deprived.

If there are many kids in your family, gift opening time might be frenzied. There might be several little tykes digging into their gifts, ripping open wrappings, paper flying around, squeals of delight, and just the regular old chaos that can be part of any family life. An autistic child who thrives on order and structure and routine might not do well.

We have certain social expectations around gift giving and gift opening. It's often expected that when a child opens a gift he must thank the person who gave it to him. Autistic kids, even those who mostly seem quite verbal, can have difficulty expressing their thoughts when they are starting to feel overwhelmed. So picking grandma out of a crowd of faces, smiling at her, and thanking her for the gift can be difficult for an autistic child. Relatives might think this is very little to ask of the kid but at that moment it might actually be more than he is able to deliver. I am not saying that courtesy should not be expected of him; of course it should, but just keep in mind that in a particular moment he might be struggling. Maybe it could be understood ahead of time that a smile and a thumbs up will do. Or he can express his thanks afterward in private.

SOMETIMES WE HAVE relatives over for the gift opening. Just the additional people, the additional noise, the additional smells can contribute to the sensory experience and an autistic child becoming overwhelmed. When adults get together they might put on a jolly persona. For some that jolliness comes with a louder than average voice, perhaps more laughing, perhaps drinking alcohol, perhaps smoking cigars or other objects that might give off strong odours.

Christmas celebrations usually involve food – more food than you might regularly eat. The lavish spread of food will create all sorts of gastric aromas as the turkey and pies are cooking. The house might be filled with smells, very good smells, but even these delicious ones can contribute to overwhelming a child's olfactory sense and be just too much.

When asking extended family to have Christmas dinner together, it is expected that everyone will sit together at a table. While your child might be quite comfortable when it's just his mom dad and siblings around, these other faces at his table can cause discomfort.

He might do actions that will help him to calm himself. He might rocked back and forth if he's sitting down, he might swing his legs (and perhaps inadvertently kick the table or someone else's chair), he might flick his fingers or flap his hands or make noises. Sometimes when an autistic child is feeling overwhelmed by auditory input – the sounds that he is hearing – he will make noises himself. It's almost as if his own noises and surpass the noises that are coming into his head so then he can cope with them more easily. But those drowning out noises can be annoying to some of the adults who just want you to make him stop.

So, what can you do? In the middle of Christmas dinner is likely not the best time to explain to great uncle Henry why your Johnny is doing whatever it is he is doing. Some of this talk should happen ahead of time. But, try as hard as you might, there will still be some relatives who just don't understand. They might not be able to comprehend all of the sensory impact that is streaming into your child's mind and body and how he might not be able to cope with this overload. Great uncle Henry will think that it never bothered him as a kid, which could very well be true. Your child is different and not everyone will understand that.

Grandparents might delight in having their entire family around them during Christmas celebration. And, it can be a nice thing, for most people. But not all.

Here are some other things that you could consider.

What is optional for you and for your child? Although relatives might expect to see your entire family at every function, perhaps you could pick and choose which ones all of you attend. Maybe seeing only part of your family on one occasion will suffice, making the next occasion easier for your child to get through.

Keep a calendar, a visual schedule posted for functions you (all of your family or just some of you) must attend. Let this schedule be readily accessible to all so that your autistic child will know what to expect.

Do as much planning ahead as possible. While some people enjoy the flurry of noise and bustle and excitement of shopping amid throngs of holiday crowds in December that level of sensory stimulation does take a toll on us all, whether or not we have autism.

Consider doing at least some of your shopping ahead of time. Those relaxing days of summer might be when you have the time and energy to think about what Aunt Susie might like. Plus, it's easier on the pocket book to space out your shopping expenditures over a number of months rather than have your credit card suffer a major assault in December.

Some social functions might dictate a certain level of attire. Think ahead of time about the clothing your child will wear and what will be most comfortable for him. A scratchy shirt, pinching new shoes or other apparel will start him off in a state of sensory tension, leaving little room for him to cope with the other inputs that might assault him or tax his ability to self-regulate.

HERE ARE some further things to think about. Is it more comfortable for your child to remain in the familiar surroundings of his own house? You could offer to host Christmas. Rather than having to leave his home where he feels safe and secure and venture into someone else's home, remaining at your place has some merit. For one thing, apart from the transition of moving into another building, his bedroom is close by where he could spend some quiet time alone.

At his aunt and uncle's home, it might be hard to find a safe place where he can retreat to regroup. But at home it is easier to help him seclude himself in his own bedroom or whatever place he finds calming where he can just chill out for a little while before coming back to join the group.

Sitting at the table in the same chair he uses every day can also lead to more of an air of familiarity then sitting at someone else's table. In some ways, it is less hassle to host Christmas at your own house. You don't have to cart presents somewhere else. You don't have to dress the kids, load them in the car and take them someplace else. It likely is more work when most of the cooking falls on your shoulders but if your child is calmer and happier that way it might make for an easier Christmas for all of you.

PREP WORK ALWAYS HELPS. Let your child know what will happen and what will be expected of him. If his grandparents and uncle and cousins are all coming over that afternoon, prepare him ahead of time. Let him know who will be there, when they're coming and what they will do when they arrive. Let him know that if he wants to he can go to his room or whatever other safe place he likes in your home when he needs to be peaceful and to calm himself. If the relatives are ones that he does not see very frequently, show pictures of who is coming. Give him stories about the person; remind him when he met them before. If other children are coming over, set some boundaries around their play. If your autistic child has a toy that he absolutely adores and absolutely cannot abide anyone else touching, this might not be the best day for a lesson in sharing. Perhaps put that toy away for today so that there won't be any squabbles over it, because your child might not be functioning at his most magnanimous on a day with all these stressors. Set up some areas where children can play and plan out some activities that they might like to do. Some of these activities might be ones your child can readily join in. Try to arrange it so that you can keep an eye on the kids playing and be ready to intervene if you think things are getting out of hand or your child needs to have a break.

You might calmly mention to the adults when they arrive that your son is tired and needs a bit of quiet time. That might be explanation enough for why he retreats to his bedroom for periods of time.

Think about tactile sensitivities; being touched is not something every child likes. In some families, it is the norm that when adults enter the home the child will go around and give each adult a hug and a kiss. If your child loves it and that is the norm in your family that's wonderful. But if your child does not enjoy that type of touch, do you think it should be his right to not have to do it? It might hurt great aunt Jane's feelings for your Johnny not to give her a welcoming hug but maybe she can get over those hurt feelings more easily than could Johnny if he was forced to endure that embrace. We teach kids about stranger danger and that they are in charge of their bodies and that is not okay for someone to touch your body at will.

IN SOME FAMILIES, everyone takes turns hosting Christmas. So, much as you might prefer to just stay home you might not have that choice. If you don't want to offend extended family members you might have to go to their home for Christmas dinner. How can you help your child?

Again, prepping him ahead of time is a good idea. Show him through pictures the people he will see there. Pictures of the person's house inside and out can help. Let him know what will happen when he gets there. Possibly the children go downstairs and play while adults watch television or work in the kitchen. If you think that your child might get overwhelmed, bring along something that is soothing to him.

Some kids love the way they feel when they're inside a tent. You can get small tents meant for young children that are pop-up variety, meaning that they open up with one good shake and when you take it down it folds neatly into a small container. Ask whoever is hosting the celebration where might be a good spot for you to set up a tent. If they think this is weird give some explanation of how your child is very sensitive to visual and auditory stimulation, how it can seem too much for him and how he can become overwhelmed. Tents are a great place to block out some of the visual stimulation and they give a sense of being cocooned in a small, safe place. Perhaps a favorite pillow can be in that tent along with a book or a soft toy that he likes to hold or fidget with. Be aware though - your child might have other cousins to whom the idea of the tent will also appeal and they might want to go in with him. That might not be a bad idea and the tent can calm kids who do not have autism.

Is there a room in the house where your child could go when he needs to have a few minutes alone to gather himself together? Asking ahead of time might give you a nice place where you can arrange this. Since this is a strange house, your child might not want to go into this unknown room on his own; he might want his mom or dad to come with him for a while.

In uncertain situations like this other things might help your child remain calm. In the sensory chapters we talked about how weight and pressure can counteract the feelings of being overwhelmed from other sensory areas. Strategies can include carrying something heavy, so he could carry chairs for you, move boxes of gifts, carry a whole stack of coats and put them on a spare bed, etc. Those are useful chores and other types of weight and heavy work can do as well. Floor push-ups, wall push-ups, pulling on his arms or legs gently or doing joint compressions might also help. This might be a time where a weighted vest would be useful. Or some ankle weights. Ankle weights can be subtle especially if they are put on underneath a pair of blue jeans; no one need even know that he has them on.

COMPRESSION VESTS CAN BE another article of clothing to consider. These are vests that, when secured with Velcro or some other type of fastener, in combination with the fabric can give a feeling of pressure around the child's torso. Some kids find garments such as Under Armour tee shirts or biker type neoprene shorts or a biker type T-shirt underneath the regular clothing might also provide a feeling of pressure that can be calming.

A WEIGHTED CUSHION on his lap during dinner might help him tolerate remaining at the table with his relatives more easily.

YOU HAVE DONE YOUR BEST; there may be some relatives who just don't get it. Ideally, you will want to catch things before your child reaches that overwhelmed state where he might either freeze or have a meltdown.

VIEWING a meltdown can be upsetting for observers, let alone how upsetting it can be for the child. Onlookers might not understand the difference between a meltdown and a tantrum. Remember, a tantrum is where the child is putting up a fuss to get something he wants. But a meltdown is a result of the sensory experience where things have built up and built up until the child just cannot handle it anymore. A tantrum will not happen in isolation; if no one is around watch the tantrum it quite quickly peters out. But a meltdown can occur no matter who is around even if the child is totally on his own.

If things reach that state it can be embarrassing. You wish your child would not do that. But, what is front and centre here is that child. It doesn't matter what anyone else thinks; what matters is how that child is feeling in the moment and his level of distress. Do what you need to do to help your child calm down. That might be removing him; it might be enveloping him in a tight hug, giving him a feeling of pressure. Keep your child foremost.

While you are tending to your child you might hear in the background comments such as he's a spoiled brat, he needs a little discipline, that wouldn't have happened back in their day, etc. Doesn't matter. Your child is your focus. You know him best and you don't want him to feel as badly as he is now.

IS HE HIGH OF LOW
FUNCTIONING?

When you learned of your child's diagnosis, there is a good chance that the terms high functioning or low functioning were included in the discussion.

While the DSM-V, the manual diagnosticians in North America most often use, does not cite these terms, the DSM does classify autism as Level One, Two or Three. These levels refer to the amount of support the child will likely require throughout their life with Level Three predicting the greater amount of support needed.

Say your child's diagnosis included the qualifier of Level One, without an intellectual disability. That means that your child's IQ fell within the average range or above. Many would then deem that child as "high functioning".

To psychologists and many educators "high functioning" refers to intelligence level. "Low functioning" would imply that that child has an intellectual disability (scores below 70 on a standardized IQ test). But it's not that simple with autism.

For one thing, it is easy to assume that a child who cannot talk has an intellectual disability. This is not a safe assumption to make. (Look at the examples given in the chapters Will He Ever Talk? And What If He Never Talks?).

Autistic kids don't do well on standardized IQ tests. The way that they process information might not fit the norms of the test. They may do poorly on the timed sections. They may come up with out-of-the box solutions to the problems posed. Their answers to the verbal questions might not be succinct and what the examiner was seeking.

Then there are autistic people who might score quite well on the IQ test but have difficulty managing the demands of their life, sometimes even more so than someone who might not have achieved scores nearly as high on the IQ test. Here is an excellent article on *Why Intelligence Scores Do Not Predict Success for Autistic Adults*[1].

How an autistic person functions can vary throughout their life, in different environments and under different stressors.

The article *What About Functioning*[2] illustrates this well.

Because of this, functioning labels can be misleading. In other chapters we've looked at examples of autistics Carly Fleischmann and Amanda Baggs. Both of these women were considered "low functioning" and severely intellectually disabled until they were given the opportunity to communicate through typing. Then they were able to demonstrate their thoughts and all that they knew. In their cases (and likely many like them) functioning labels did harm by creating assumptions about these women. For more on this, please take a look at this short piece: *Functioning Labels: Why You Shouldn't Be Using Them*[3].

If a person receives the label of "high functioning" there is the presumption that that person can manage well on their own. Accommodations might not be offered when indeed they would have made a vast difference in that person's life.

"The difference between high-functioning autism and low-functioning is that high-functioning means your deficits are ignored, and low-functioning means your assets are ignored," by Laura Tisoncik.

This concern about labels is raised over and over by autistic adults. *Please Listen to Autistic People*[4].

## IS HE LAZY?

Is your child lazy? Well, sometimes, but then, aren't we all? But before you label certain behaviors as simply lazy, let's look at what else might be going on.

Some autistic adults use the term "autistic inertia". It's like a form of procrastination. Think about when you procrastinate. When *I* procrastinate it could be for several reasons:

- It's a non-preferred task and I'd just rather be doing something else.
- I'm not quite sure how to do it so am avoiding that state of insecurity when I have to stumble around, trying to figure it out.
- There's a deadline looming, and this just has to be done, but the task seems too enormous.

- It matters and if I mess it up, the consequences will not be good.
- I've had trouble with this in the past, didn't like that feeling so am trying to get out of doing it.

This is just a partial list; we all procrastinate at times. When you're autistic, all these same reasons may apply, on top of some other possibilities.

Has your child failed at something similar before? The emotional barriers could be blocking her from trying again. Many autistic kids have faced social failure time and time again. How do you put yourself out there when it's hurt so much in the past?

COMMUNICATION IS a weak area for everyone on the autism spectrum, no matter how verbal they may seem. Even though you've given the direction over and over again, do they truly understand what is expected of them? Were they paying attention to your words or were they focusing on something else? Even though you assume that they know that this is a regular part of their routine, do they actually know this? This is the time to back up words with visuals - either pictures or written instructions. It's easier to take in and process visual information rather than oral.

Set up routines and yes, back up these routines with a visual schedule. Does your child procrastinate about setting the table? Write it into his schedule for a specific time. Are you quite picky about the placement of the cutlery? Make a visual he can follow. (A piece of paper resembling a place mat would do, with the plate, glass, cutlery, etc. drawn in the spots you want them to go). The more things you can make routine the easier his day (and yours) will go.

Do not just assume that because you always do things this way or in this order that he has picked up on your routine. Use visuals. This includes not just creating the visual but teaching what it is and referring to it often. Demonstrate how you go look at your schedule to see what you need to do next. Let him see you using your To Do list and your shopping list.

THIS BRINGS us to the subject of executive functioning. These are key skills that we need to manage our lives. Executive functioning includes our time sense, our ability to prioritize and to organize. It includes our ability to ignore distractors and to persist at a task. If you have great difficulty organizing yourself, tasks can seem monumental, making it easy to give up or not even try. You can help by breaking tasks into smaller pieces, writing those down and stroking a line through each as it is completed. (Again, don't just talk about it, but show it visually). Is there an essay or book report due? Chunk the component tasks along a timeline, with dates for when each part is to be tackled. Depending on the assignment, you might help him choose a topic by Monday, Tuesday write down all the subtopics that might be interesting about that topic. The next day, research and jot down notes about 2 of these topics, etc. If your child is technologically inclined, you might prefer to use an app or software program for this.

If you do an online search for mind mapping, you will find many options for a phone, tablet or computer. One example for young students is Kidspiration[1]. If you're new to the concept of mind mapping here[2] is an explanation. Here are *8 free mind mapping tools*[3] and ways to use them. MindMup[4] is a free, online mind mapping tool. The best mind mapping tools of 2019 are described in this article[5].

Executive functioning skills include a sense of time. If someone tells you that they'll meet you in 10 minutes, likely you have an internal sense of how long 10 minutes is, even if you do not look at a watch. Having this sense of the passage of time can be a weak area for many autistic people. If an essay is due in two weeks, without that sense of time, the student could have little idea that a week and a half has gone by already. Teaching calendar skills can help. Talk about the calendar together, how the days of the week are listed across the top and how each number represents a day. (Believe me; this is not obvious to all kids). Cross off each day before bed to help him get a sense of the passage of time.

SENSORY ISSUES INTERFERE seriously with the lives of many autistic people. Most neurotypicals (those without a specific diagnosis) have good central coherence - the ability to weed out of the environment that which we don't need to pay attention to. But for those on the autism spectrum, often all the sensory inputs from the environment come at them with the same intensity. It takes a lot of concentration to consciously recognize then choose to not attend to all those incoming, pesky messages. The hum of the air conditioning needs to be ignored even though it is just as prominent as the words you're saying to them. The dust particles from sun beams coming through the window partially obscure your face, making it difficult to look at you. The seam along the right toe of his sock is rubbing against his sneaker, irritating him and distracting his thoughts. As you can imagine, such a sensory load can make it hard to pay attention or even cause a person to freeze up. Or, understandably, to avoid certain situations or tasks.

OVERWHELMED AND EXHAUSTED. Yes, that is often how autistic people feel. Just getting through the day can take all of their energy. You can see how they would need more down time than might someone else their age.

So, lazy? Perhaps sometimes. But more often what on the surface may look like laziness is really a reaction to weak executive functioning skills and all the influences that they are struggling with.

You can help by:

- creating routines,
- using visuals,
- breaking tasks into pieces,
- teaching organizational strategies,
- understanding his sensory issues and providing supports (see the chapter on sensory for more ideas),

- allowing for down time, and
- finding the relaxation strategies that work for him.

SARA HARVEY IS an articulate autistic woman who frankly and clearly explains aspects of autism to us. Listen[6] to her views on autism, depression and inertia.

# WILL HE BE ABLE TO LIVE ON HIS OWN?

 hapter Twenty-Nine -

WILL he be able to live on his own? Good question. That depends on him (or her) and on you as their parents.

You see, there is a wide spectrum of abilities among autistic people. Roughly half of those diagnosed with autism have cognitive ability (or IQs) in the average to above average range. And, about half have some degree of intellectual disability ranging from mild to profound. Many people with mild intellectual disabilities and perhaps some with moderate ID are able to live independently with varying degrees of assistance.

There are definitely those who have both autism and an intellectual disability but determining those is not clear cut. You see, we determine level of intellectual functioning by using intelligence tests. The most common one you might hear of is the WISC (Wechsler Intelligence Scale for Children) or the WAIS (Wechsler Adult Intelligence Scale). They look at various ways we think and reason, including our working memory, processing speed, verbal comprehension and perceptual reasoning.

As you are aware, some people on the autism spectrum are nonverbal and cannot use speech for communication. Others are more able to express themselves using words sometimes, but when anxious or becoming overwhelmed, the use of speech is more difficult for them.

The problem with intelligence tests and autism is that some of the test parts require verbal skills, meaning that the individual has to be answer orally. There are some ways around this and a nonverbal (not requiring spoken responses) form can be given. This somewhat takes care of the verbal requirement, but there is still another problem.

Even if the speech requirement is removed, or with those who do communicate orally, when taking an IQ test, the individual must be able to understand what the examiner says and what is required of them. While hearing might not be a problem, auditory processing often is. Although the person can hear just fine, making sense of the words he hears may not always be easy. Auditory processing is more difficult under noisy, disruptive conditions but intellectual assessments are usually conducted in a quiet atmosphere.

The ability to process is also affected by anxiety and the testing situation itself is anxiety-producing. Often the test is conducted by a stranger in an unfamiliar room. The process itself is intimidating.

If those factors are all fine for the person being tested, there is pacing. Many autistics trying to make sense of things, find that the world moves at a fast pace - too fast for their comfort. By the time they have worked out what is going on and what may be expected of them, others have moved on to the next thing. Parts of the IQ tests are timed with bonus points for finishing more quickly and lower points being awarded (or penalized) for those who take beyond the expected seconds or minutes to complete the task.

An autistic mind might not travel along the same path as that of the neurotypical examiner. While there are certain sets of questions and items to go through, in a certain order, the autistic person being examined might not follow along. Something the examiner says or asks, or part of the test might take the testee's mind down a different avenue, something of interest to that person - something far more interesting than the task the tester has set out. Time may be lost as the person focuses on something that caught his fancy and he may miss instructions, complete a task in the wrong way or lose out on timed points.

Many people on the autism spectrum have difficulty with executive functioning. EF skills involve such things as our sense of time, our ability to maintain our focus and to shift attention appropriately. EF involves other things, but these particularly affect performance on an intellectual assessment.

Fatigue also sets in. Undergoing such testing is not fun and is fatiguing for anyone. But if you are autistic and must put in extra effort to control your attention and play along with someone else's agenda for hours, it will become hard to maintain focus. None of us perform at our best when tired and/or anxious.

This is a very long way of saying that while intelligence tests are the best measures we have right now to assess level of intellectual functioning, they have flaws and are not necessarily accurate with the autistic population.

ARE you wondering when we will get to whether or not your child will be able to live on his own? We're getting there.

It depends partly on his level of intellectual functioning. Someone with a profound intellectual disability will require a much higher degree of care all his life than someone whose ability is closer to the average range.

But IQ alone will not determine if an individual can live independently. As we discussed above, the scores from an IQ test may not tell the full story of how a person functions.

There are autistic people who, when young, presented as if they had an intellectual disability, but later in life this was clearly not true. Temple Grandin is an example. Sometimes individuals who are nonverbal and unable to use spoken language to communicate their wants and needs might come across as lower functioning. A few other examples are Stephen Shore[1], Carly Fleischmann[2] and Amanda Baggs[3].

My advice is to never assume. Never

assume that your child is incapable or does not understand. I find it sad when adults talk about a child in his presence as if he cannot hear nor understand what they are saying. It's rude. Even if the child does not understand the words, he might pick up on your tone or attitude. But what if he *does* understand but just can't communicate that to you? There are instances of adults who are now articulate in some form (verbally or in writing) who can recall what was said about them in front of them when they were children.

I am not implying that hiding inside every autistic person is a budding genius. This is not true of the general population and neither is it true among those with autism. But the way your child seems to you at age 4 when you compare him to other preschoolers is not necessarily the way he will be compared to his peers at age 14 or 24 or 34. Don't assume. And by that, I mean don't assume *anything*.

Now, let's skip ahead a decade or two. Your child's time in the school system is coming to a close. You wonder if he will live under your roof forever.

It is unlikely that he will finish his stint in high school then move out of his own to begin his adult life at age 18. Or, if he does, it might not be successful. (Again, there are no rules. This will depend on how prepared your offspring is). Many typical young adults find the move to adult life difficult, but this is even more true of those on the autism spectrum.

An abrupt transition from living under his parents' care to taking up the reins of adult life independently is a huge step that many young people struggle with. The difficulty and stress would be multiplied vastly if your adult child has autism.

Instead, begin early, way early. Adolescence may even be late to begin looking toward adult life.

Think of the skills needed to live life on a day-to-day basis then begin teaching those. When young, give your child the ability to make choices, starting with the clothes he puts on, etc. Hold him accountable for his choices, helping him to see the pros and cons of the options.

Give him responsibilities; everyone in the home can contribute to the functioning of the house in some way. Responsibilities increase as the child ages.

Do not do for the child something he can do for himself. Yes, it takes longer, and the result might not look as pretty but learning independence is crucial.

Once at a conference I chatted with a mom whose son would be attending college in a few months. She was so enthused and proud of her son's ability. His college had a residential program for autistic and learning disabled students; we were here to listen to their presentation. The college reps talked about the accommodations and assistance they'd extend to students in their program. At the end of the talk this mom raised a hand and asked a question, "But who will do his laundry?" There was silence. Oh dear. I appreciate that she was so proud of her son's intelligence and high grade point average. But what is the point of being smart if you don't have the life skills to be able to do anything with those smarts?

Laundry is one of those pesky management things we all need to do. It's a skill that can easily be taught, especially when enhanced by visuals. Even young children can help transfer clothes from the washing machine to the dryer.

I met the parents of a young autistic woman who was thirty. She had successfully completed high school, a Bachelor's degree at university and then a Master's degree in music. But her self-management skills were woefully lacking. Lucky for her, her parents were well off financially. They described to me what they had in place. They bought her a three-bedroom condo. One bedroom was for their daughter, the second was her music room and the third, along with its en-suite was for the paid companion who resided there to take care of their daughter.

They had a variety of other part-time employers to assist this young woman. One did all her grocery shopping, clothing and personal shopping and her laundry. A housekeeper came in daily to clean and to cook. Another woman arrived early each morning to get their daughter out of bed, coax her through dressing, hygiene and breakfast then took the bus with her to her part-time job. Once there, a job coach took over, spending four hours with her as she performed clerical work in an office. Then, the morning woman returned at noon to accompany the daughter on the bus back home. A trust fund was set up to continue this assistance permanently.

Not many of us are in financial positions to be able to spend this degree on money. Was it necessary? Her parents definitely believed so. They did not think she was capable of acquiring any of these skills on her own despite having been able to complete a advanced degree at university. I wonder....

Most kids will need to acquire some degree of independent and self-management skills. Even those who will reside in a group home will be expected to contribute to the running of the house.

A few examples of skills that can be taught are:
- how to organize and clean your bedroom
- how to wash dishes
- how to cook
- how to shop for groceries
- how to budget money
- how to clean a house
- how to open and manage a bank account and/or credit card

WHEN OUR CHILD IS DIFFERENT, there is a tendency to over-protect. We know that life is harder for him and want to do what we can to help. Sometimes that urge to protect takes the form of doing things for him. While kind, providing "good care" might not be what he needs. Opportunities to learn how to care for himself might be more valuable.

What is the point of being smart if you can't manage your life enough so that you can make use of those smarts?

"We have seen many individuals whose natural talents are wasted due to their untreated social disability and other weaknesses (e.g. inability to manage the practical aspects of independent living." Klin, Volkmar & Sparrow. *Asperger Syndrome* (2002), p. 8.

Read or listen to the thoughts these autistic adults have on this:

- Stephen Shore[1]
- Carly Fleischmann[2]
- Amanda Baggs[3]

## WILL HE BE ABLE TO HOLD DOWN A JOB?

Will he be able to hold down a job? That is another good question and like many of the others, it depends. Much of it depends on the individual's level of functioning as well as the skills he has acquired.

Level of functioning applies to a number of different things. In psychological terms, level of functioning often refers to cognitive ability or IQ level. (We covered some of this in the previous chapter. If you read that, then you might want to skip to the next section of this chapter to see how it applies to the world of work).

IQ stands for intellectual quotient. This is usually derived from a standardized IQ test. Some of the most common IQ tests are the Weschler Adult Intelligence Scale (WAIS) for people age 16 and up and for kids the

Weschler Intelligence Scale for Children (WISC) is used.

While very few people will say that these are exact and accurate measures of a person's intelligence, for now they're the best tool that we have. But for people on the autism spectrum the results are even more suspicious. It's not uncommon to meet autistic people who have scored quite low on one of the Weschler IQ tests yet when people work with them; they see skills that would not be expected for someone functioning at that low of a level.

Some of the difficulties with IQ tests and people with autism are related to their language ability. Some autistic people are nonverbal, meaning that they don't use spoken words to communicate. They might communicate quite well through some sort of assistive technology or typing or gestures or a picture system but not by talking. About half of the subtests involved in a Weschler IQ test require spoken responses. Now, some clinicians do administer a Weschler allowing non-spoken responses. For example, the person might type out what they want to say. This is breaking the standardization of the test so the results are somewhat suspect, but at least it gives you an indication of how that person might be thinking and how they respond to the test items.

Even with those individuals who do speak there might be other language problems. You need the ability to understand what is said to you in order to follow the oral directions on the Weschler tests. Some people are able to grasp of the requirements by watching the demonstrations with the physical materials but understanding what is said orally would make that much easier.

Timing is another aspect. Some of the items on the Weschler are timed responses meaning that the individual must respond within a certain amount of time in order to get points for that question. And there are bonus points for responding promptly and accurately.

Many autistic people have difficulties with executive functioning and with processing speed so they may understand the task but comply slowly, it may take them a while to figure out what is required, but in the end they can do it accurately. Still others will have difficulty understanding what the examiner says.

Also, along with executive functioning is the ability to manage attention. This can be problematic for some autistic people. For one, it requires joint attention which has the examiner and the examinee both focusing their attention on the same thing at the same time. Some people being tested are more observant of their own internal thoughts which may not run along the line of what the test is requiring hence slowing down their response or having them not respond at all. For example, if the person has an inner dialogue or monologue running and the examiner asks a question that requires a spoken response, the person might give a response that is based on the thoughts in his own mind rather than the response the examiner requests.

Some people with an autism diagnosis legitimately also has a diagnosis of an intellectual disability that might range from profound to mild. Most people with a severe or profound intellectual disability are not engaged in paid work. That does not necessarily mean that they don't contribute in any fashion. Some people residing in group homes who require a considerable amount of daily care, also contribute in those group homes by doing chores such as setting the table, emptying the dishwasher, etc.

It is generally assumed that the higher the IQ, the higher the potential the individual has for learning and later on for working. Now, it certainly is not a black-and-white line here and there are many, many variables

Back to the terms low functioning and high functioning. (We spent some time on this in a previous chapter but will go over it briefly in case you skipped that chapter).

There is quite a controversy within the autism community about this. There are those individuals who are supposedly deemed low functioning who in fact functioned internally at a much higher level than people would expect. Examples of this are Amanda Baggs[1] and Carly Fleischmann[2].

Even those people on the autism spectrum who are deemed "high functioning" often readily admit that they are not high functioning in all aspects every day. It can change and change quickly and unpredictably. Most often this has to do with anxiety and/or sensory sensitivities. Someone may manage to hold together under ordinary circumstances but then something comes along that impacts their sensory sensitivities hugely so that they feel overwhelmed. Then, while in that state, they are no longer able to function at a high level, meaning their normal coping mechanisms and skills for managing themselves, keeping their emotions and reactions regulated and just functioning in their day-to-day life are greatly diminished.

But it is in just such an environment that some autistic adults are finding success. Chef Tom Dickinson[3] is an example. So, as always with autism, never assume. Let the person be guided by his interests and skills.

There are some jobs that carry with them the requirement of socialization. This could be trying for many on the autism spectrum. While someone with autism might be friendly and have the need for a certain number of friendly encounters, nonstop rubbing shoulders with other people can be challenging. (And not just for those who have autism).

Processing speed enters into this as well. If you are going to be a receptionist in a busy office, you must be able to multitask well and do it all rapidly. You might be required to man the phones, operating several different lines at the same time, keeping track of whom you have put on hold, which caller you are transferring to and take down any required messages. That can be a stress-producing situation for many people. On the other hand, if someone can manage the pace and multitasking, in that job the individual's social contacts with others might be limited in both time and the quality of interactions. The interactions might require courtesy and speed and a short number of sentences but that's all, which could suit some employees.

This new world of online commerce and contract work is a real boon for many on the autism spectrum. They can work from home, maybe even in their pyjamas, and often at whatever hours suit them. The drawback to such contract work is that rarely does it come with the benefits such as health care pension etc. And it requires a certain degree of multitasking because while you're working on one contract you need to be always chasing the next one so that you will have some work lined up for when you have completed the first job. If someone has the executive functioning skills to manage, this working from home can be ideal.

Many people who have an autism diagnosis and post-secondary education are under-employed. This means that they are likely not doing a job that requires the skills and knowledge that they obtained during their post- secondary training. There are a couple reasons for this.

It's one thing to be able to do well in an academic setting, acquiring and demonstrating those skills. It's another thing to be able to carry those skills into the work environment. Some find the work part of it just too stressful and choose to than take a job that requires not as much thinking power, concentration, socialization, organization, etc.

There's another reason why some of these bright, competent autistic adults are not working in their trained fields. The thing is, first they have to land the job. And in most situations, you land that job initially through an interview.

The interview process is not an easy one for most autistic individuals. Interviews require a lot of reading between the lines trying to determine what exactly the interviewer is getting at and what he would he like you to say. Often interview questions are open-ended leaving the interviewee unsure of what is wanted or the direction in which the questions are heading. So, the job candidate might give what he believes is a full answer but in doing so talk on and on and on, boring the interviewer or not allowing the company person to get another question in. "Full disclosure" to an autistic person might mean exactly that and he will confess to every error he has ever made. In his effort to be as accommodating and forthright as he could, he might have lost himself the job. Having a portfolio of work to take along can be really helpful because then the company can see examples of exactly what the person is capable of.

There are a few other difficulties autistic people will face when getting a job. Let me give you an example. A dad once said to me about his young adult son, "he won't do anything he doesn't want to. He won't do anything he doesn't see the point of." Then he went on to explain that "see the point of" means something that's meaningful and interesting to his son.

Any of you who hold a job know that no matter how much you might enjoy the work and enjoy the challenges, there will be parts of that job that you do not enjoy. That's just part of life; there are things that we all have to do that we do not feel like doing but must get done anyway. It's the rare person who gets to do only what they want to do.

Well I certainly understand this dad's point of view and the fact that his son only wants to do those things that interest him. Sadly, life just does not work that way. So, this young man is not able to hold down a job, not even a part-time job. He wants to just pick the parts of a task that appeal to him and appeal to him at that particular moment; what appeals varies day-to-day. That's likely true of most of us, but then there is the "suck it up factor". We just have to do certain things whether or not we like them or whether or not we feel like it at the present time; they still need to get done, because that's just part of the whole parcel.

I hear this in schools as well when we're talking about autistic students. I've been a teacher and I know many teachers. Most try very hard to make their life and their assignments as interesting as possible but sadly, it is not possible to appeal to everyone all of the time. And there are just things that need to get done. In school there are ways to modify and offer alternatives, still, there are times when you are expected to do something whether or not it appeals you. That's also a fact in the working world.

Not being able to do things whether or not you feel like it can be a real hindrance with finding and keeping a job. You may have heard of PDA. PDA stands for Pathological Demand Avoidance. While this is not a diagnostic label in any of our medical books, it is a term used by some parents and other professionals working with kids who have autism. These children do not react well to being told what to do. This is not the place to debate whether PDA actually exists as an entity on its own or whether it's a combination of anxiety, mindset etc., nonetheless, the manifestations of the problem exist.

In a workplace most people are given orders; they are told what to do by a supervisor and the expectation is that they will comply with those orders without arguing, without pitching a fit and without delay. If you are unable to do those things the odds are you will not keep your job very long.

THERE ARE young adults on the autism spectrum who have not and likely never will attend post-secondary school. Can they hold down jobs? Perhaps.

Again, this will depend on their ability level, their attitude, their desire and the training or practice they have received. There are autistic young people who have jobs stocking shelves. For some they might work in large department stores on the night shift. The advantage of this is that there are few or no customers in the store who could interrupt them by asking where things are. They might get to work in a quieter environment and more at their own pace. If they are an exact type of person they might enjoy lining things up properly on the shelves, putting things in the proper order, and at the end of the shift having completed the tasks that were signed.

I know a young woman who was stocking shelves quite capably during the day but would become very frustrated with the customers would come right behind her and make a mess of her nicely organized shelf. She wanted to tell them to leave things alone and put things back, and not to touch. That was not the job for her.

Being out in the world, rubbing shoulders with other people, and trying to block out the sensory stimuli that might be bombarding them can be very fatiguing. Going home and having some down time can be absolutely crucial. For this reason, some autistic people feel more successful when they have only a part-time job, which allows them more down time.

WHILE IT MIGHT SEEM that you focus on your child's challenges and "deficits", there are some positives about being autistic than can make someone a great employee. Here are just a few:

- Many autistic people excel at technical skills. Even if they are not seeking a tech-related job, so many types of employment require a high level of technical, computer-related skills.
- The ability of hyper focus can be a wondrous thing. When engaged in a task many autistics can be totally engrossed and dedicated to what they are doing.
- When your child is not doing what you want, you might see this characteristic as stubbornness. But often in adult life, tenacity is a much-needed trait.

- Tenacity and the ability to hyper focus might suit long work hours or flexible work environments when the goal is to complete a task, then have some down time.
- Although the inability to see the forest for the trees can be an impediment sometimes, such attention to detail might be just what an employer is seeking.
- One downside of some work situations is office gossip. Most autistics will have zero interest in this type of socializing and may not pick up on innuendos and undercurrents.

THE BLOG *Every Day Aspie*[4] lists these *10 Considerations for the Autistic Workforce*[5].

1. Anxiety
2. Sensory Processing
3. Communication
4. Socializing
5. Misunderstood and Misinterpretations
6. Knowing What to Expect and Order
7. Feedback

8. Over Work/Under Work
9. Silence and Alone Time
10. Processing Spoken and Written Information

As for career choices, well that is a huge question. What type of a job the person might seek and enjoy depends on his or her interests and talents.

It might be assumed that some environments are not good for people on the autism spectrum. Many get easily overwhelmed by sensory inputs. To me a busy commercial kitchen would seem like one of the worst environments. They are noisy, they're busy, there's all kinds of movement with people and utensils whizzing around the room. There are smells of all sorts. Workers in a commercial kitchen have to move at a hectic pace which would prove stressful for many, many people. But it is in just such an environment that some autistic adults are finding success such as Chef Tom Dickinson mentioned above. Another example is Chef Chris Fischer[6].

So, as always with autism, never assume. Let the person be guided by his interests and skills.

So, bottom line. Can your autistic child hold down a job when he's an adult? Likely. That depends on some of the variables we've already discussed here

The biggest failures that I see are when the preparation has not been done. Sometimes just getting the child through the school system can seem like a huge task. And it is, don't let anyone tell you otherwise. With most typical kids they finish school and have within them a desire to move out and begin their life on their own, whether that's in the world of work or attending a postsecondary program. The change does not come easily for those who have autism. While typical kids listen to what their peers are doing and they catch that bug about moving out on their own, that might not happen when a kid is autistic. For one, they might not pick up on the social nuances that say it would not be cool to remain living with your parents. For another thing, that whole moving out business is pretty darn scary.

Think about it. Think of when you first left home. There's the business of finding a place to live, getting the money for a down payment or for a damage deposit, plus the first month's rent. Then once you're in your own place, what do you do? How do you get furniture? How do you feed yourself? What do you cook on? These things can all be overwhelming for any young person but if you have autism, it can seem insurmountable. So, preparation starts years and years ahead. A decade early is by no means too soon. Start with chores and responsibilities around the house. I don't mean that your eight-year-old should be a slave to housework, but that eight-year-old can certainly contribute. At that age he can do some of the vacuuming he can load or unload the dishwasher, set the table, and many, many other things that he can do to contribute to the well-being of the family. By early teen years most kids can, with assistance, do laundry. The more that a kid has experience with at home the easier it will be for him to manage himself later on.

## WILL HE...?

Will he have friends?
Will he get married?
Who will look out for him when I'm gone?

There are still so many questions, aren't there? Your crystal ball is murky, and no one can predict just how things will look for your child in another decade or two or three.

Chapters twenty-seven to thirty will give you some ideas on ways you can prepare your child for his future. This is just the beginning and each individual's path will be different and follow its own timeline. Be patient. Be persistent. Be positive and supportive. Your child *will* progress.

# NOTE FROM THE AUTHOR

I love hearing from readers, and I promise to reply. In fact, the premises from the novels in the Autism School Daze series (as well as those soon to be published) all came from readers. Thanks, guys!

Have an idea you'd like to see in another book? I'd love to hear from you.

Interested in autism? In kids who learn differently and those who support them? Sign up for the newsletter and join in the conversation.

## NOTE FROM THE AUTHOR

Contact the author at questions@drsharonmitchell.org.

Follow Dr. Mitchell on:

Twitter - http://www.twitter.com/autismsite
Facebook - http://www.facebook.com/drsharonamitchell
Pinterest - https://www.pinterest.ca/mitchellsha3047/
Instagram - https://www.instagram.com/autismsite/
Website - http://www.drsharonmitchell.org/

Sign up for her newsletter at http://drsharonmitchell.org/newsletter.

ENJOYED THIS BOOK?

Thank you for spending your valuable time with this book. If you have enjoyed it the author would be greatly appreciative if you would leave a review at the retailer where you purchased the book. Reviews mean a lot to authors and they are the way that new readers discover the work. (If you're not sure how to leave a review, contact the author at the link below and she'll be happy to show you how to do it.)

Author Dr. Sharon Mitchell loves connecting with readers. Contact her through her website at http://www.drsharonmitchell.org. There you will find information on her other books, her workshop appearances and questions families and teachers often ask about kids who have autism spectrum disorders.

## ENJOYED THIS BOOK?

Would you like to join the author's review team? Team members receive complimentary, advance copies of each new title. Contact Sharon at http://www.drsharonmitchell.org.

## ABOUT THE AUTHOR

Dr. Sharon A. Mitchell has a Ph.D. in Psychology Management, specializing in autism spectrum disorders. Her Master's work looked at the long-term outlook for young people with Asperger's Syndrome and high functioning autism. Her career has been spent as a consultant, counsellor and special education teacher.

She has presented to thousands of participants in workshops and conferences. Her passion is helping those who are autistic and the people who support them.

She is also author of the books in the School Daze series, all available on your favorite online booksellers. You can also ask for them in libraries and bookstores.

When she is not writing, you'll find her farming, working on yard projects or welding.

You can reach Dr. Mitchell at questions@dr-sharonmitchell.org, at her website http://www.drsharonmitchell.org or on social media at these links:

Twitter - http://www.twitter.com/autismsite
Facebook - http://www.facebook.com/drsharonamitchell
Pinterest - https://www.pinterest.ca/mitchellsha3047/
Instagram - https://www.instagram.com/autismsite/
Website - http://www.drsharonmitchell.org/

## OTHER BOOKS IN THE SERIES

There's more! If you liked *Autism Questions Parents Ask,* the other books in the Autism Help series might be useful:

- *Autism Questions Teachers Ask* (available September 15, 2019)
- *Autism and the Dental Office* (available November 15, 2019)

You might also enjoy the novels in the autism School Daze series. Each portrays a different child who has an autism spectrum disorder. Many of the same characters appear in each book.

*Autism Goes to School*
*Autism Runs Away*
*Autism Belong*
*Autism Talks and Talks*

## OTHER BOOKS IN THE SERIES

*Autism Grows Up*

And coming soon:

*The Autism Goes to School Workbook*
*Jeff's Story - Prequel to Autism Goes to School*

Next, here's a synopsis of each book. Sample chapters of each one are available at http://www.drsharonmitchell.org.

# SYNOPSIS OF NOVELS IN THE AUTISM SCHOOL DAZE SERIES

***Autism Goes to School***

We're thrilled to announce that this Amazon bestseller is also a Human Relations and B.R.A.G. Medallion winner!

After suddenly receiving custody of his five-year-old son, Ben must learn how to be a dad. The fact that he'd even fathered a child was news to him. Not only does this mean restructuring his sixty-hour workweek and becoming responsible for another human being, but also Kyle has an autism diagnosis.

Enter the school system and a shaky beginning. Under the guidance of a gifted teacher, Ben and Kyle take tentative steps to becoming father and son.

Teacher Melanie Nicols sees Ben as a deadbeat dad, but grudgingly comes to admire how he hangs in, determined to learn for his son's sake. Her admiration grows to more as father and son come to rely on Melanie being a part of their lives.

When parents receive the news that their child has autism, they spend countless hours researching the subject, usually at night, after an exhausting day. Teachers, when they hear that they'll have a student with an autism spectrum disorder, also try to learn as much as they can. This novel was written for such parents and teachers - an entertaining read that offers information on autism and strategies that work.

Find it at your favorite retailer at https://Books2Read.com/AutismGoestoSchool.

### *Autism Runs Away*

Ethan is only in grade one and already has been *kicked out of one school* due to his tantrums and pattern of running away when in a panic. Now, his mom has enrolled him in a new school but remains glued to her phone, waiting for the call to tell her to come pick him up, that they can't handle him, that they don't know what to do with a child who has **autism**.

How can she trust these strangers to look after her son, just one small child among hundreds, when he has run from own parents so very many times? They don't know the terror of losing your child in a mall or watching him run blindly into traffic.

What started as a fun chase game when Ethan was a toddler has turned into a terrifying deviation. The adults in his life never know when he might take off.

Rather than attaching an adult to his side to keep him safe, this new teacher talks about calming strategies and choices. Do they not realize what could happen if Ethan flees the building? The impact of a car on one small body? Sara is about to learn if this new school is up to the challenge.

Meet Kyle, Mel, Ben and the other characters you got to know in the award-winning bestseller *Autism Goes to School*. See what they've been up to in the last year and how they join forces to help Ethan.

Then, return to Madson School to see if Manny, a child with severe autism belongs in their midst. Read Manny's story in *Autism Belongs*.

Find it at your favorite retailer at https://Books2Read.com/AutismRunsAway.

*Autism Belongs*

Manny is not like other children. He doesn't talk. He doesn't leave the house. His parents desperately try to arrange their world so that Manny does not get upset. Because, when he does, well, the aggression was getting worse. Too many times Tomas had to leave work to rescue his wife from the havoc of their son's meltdowns. At ten, Manny was becoming difficult to handle.

Passing by a bakery made all the difference. There, they met people who understand autism, along with its strengths and challenges. They learn ways to help Manny communicate and socialize and to have his needs met.

Dare they consider letting him go to school? Is there a chance that Manny actually **belongs** there? You bet.

Meet Kyle, Ben, Mel and the other

characters you read about in the award-winning bestseller ***Autism Goes to School*** and see how they've grown and progressed.

Find it at your favorite retailer at https://Books2Read.com/AutismBelongs.

***Autism Talks and Talks***

Karen is bright, vivacious and highly verbal. Perhaps too verbal. She finds certain topics fascinating and goes on and on and on not realizing she has bored her audience. She remains on the fringe, looking at other adolescents having fun together and wondering if she could ever be a part of the group. Karen has **Asperger's Syndrome**.

Who best to help her but an **autistic chef**? *What?!*

Yep! Meet Jeff. His special talents and view of the world are just what Karen needs. And, Jeff learns that he is just what one particular woman needs as well.

Is this all there is for Karen? Will an autistic man find the love he didn't know he was seeking? Come join us and see.

Find it at your favorite retailer at https://Books2Read.com/AutismTalksandTalks.

*Autism Grows Up*

At twenty-one, Suzie has withdrawn from a world she finds alien and confusing. She has

Asperger's Syndrome as well as high anxiety. To her, the world is a harsh, scary place where she does not fit.

She spends much of her days sleeping and most of her nights on the computer. Her mother, Amanda, wishes Suzie would get a job, go to school or at least help out around the house. Suzie feels that her time is amply filled with the compelling world lurking within her computer.

Amanda wants more for Suzie but does not know how to help her move forward. When she tries putting pressure on her, Suzie suffers from paralyzing anxiety, resulting in morose withdrawal or worse, lengthy tantrums.

Suzie is most content when alone in the basement with her computer. Staring at her monitor, the rest of the world falls away and she feels at home.

Amanda is torn. She met this gentleman, Jack. It would be nice to spend time with someone other than her brother and daughter, but Suzie wouldn't like it and needs her mother desperately. Jack gently persists and Amanda glimpses what her life could be like.

Uncomfortable questions arise like what will become of Suzie if something happens to Amanda? But when an intruder breaks into the house, Amanda has only Suzie to rely on.

Find it at your favorite retailer at https://Books2Read.com/AutismGrowsUp.

*Autism Goes to School*
*Autism Runs Away*
*Autism Belongs*
*Autism Talks and Talks*
*Autism Grows Up*

Coming soon:

*Prequel to Autism Goes to School - Jeff's Story*
*The Autism Goes to School Workbook*
*Autism Questions Teachers Ask*
(Release date September 15, 2019)

*Autism and the Dental Office*
(Release date November 15, 2019)

# WHAT PEOPLE SAY ABOUT DR. MITCHELLS BOOKS AND PRESENTATIONS

- "A gem of a book"
- " A true delight - Highly, highly recommended
- Just couldn't put it down"
- "Highly informative and extremely helpful - Couldn't take my eyes off it"
- I loved this book from beginning to end - Just plain awesome
- I could feel the author's passion - What a great way to learn about autism
- "Entertains, entrances & educates: 3 for the price of one!"
- "This wonderful book is about a Dad, Ben, meeting his autistic son Kyle for the very first time, when Mom dumps him suddenly on his doorstep, saying she can no longer take care of him. Through the eyes of Ben, we get a glimpse of both the challenges and joys of

being a parent of a child who sees the world in different ways."

•"Unlike some stories that speak of autistic children, this one brings a wealth of hope and information! As we look over Ben's shoulder, we see a glimpse of the learning tools currently being used in the classroom today, and we get glimpses of things that could be helpful in the day to day life of an autistic child."

•"I appreciated this story on several levels. First, I enjoyed the story of Ben discovering what it means to be a parent, especially a single parent. Second, I enjoyed watching Kyle find his own means of success in this new and upside- down world. "

•"I enjoyed the glimpse into classroom life and options available today. Finally I enjoyed the quiet romance between Mel and Ben."

# NOTES

## HOW TO USE THIS BOOK

1. https://Books2Read.com/AutismGoestoSchool
2. https://Books2Read.com/AutismRunsAway
3. https://Books2Read.com/AutismBelongs
4. https://Books2Read.com/AutismTalksandTalks
5. https://Books2Read.com/AutismGrowsUp
6. https://Books2Read.com/AutismQuestionsParentsAsk
7. https://Books2Read.com/AutismQuestionsTeachersAsk

## 2. WHAT KIND OF THERAPIES ARE OUT THERE?

1. https://themighty.com/2017/02/aba-therapy-autistic-perspective/
2. https://autisticmama.com/big-deal-aba-therapy/
3. https://www.spectrumnews.org/features/deep-dive/controversy-autisms-common-therapy/
4. https://theautismcafe.com/en/a-balanced-view-on-aba-therapy-by-an-autistic-adult/
5. https://autisticuk.org/does-aba-harm-autistic-people/
6. https://the-art-of-autism.com/how-i-teach-autistic-students-without-using-aba/
7. https://www.webmd.com/diet/features/diet-and-autism#1
8. https://www.webmd.com/brain/autism/gluten-free-casein-free-diets-for-autism#1
9. https://autism.org/treatment-old/gluten-and-casein-free-diets/
10. http://www.thinkingautismguide.-

## NOTES

com/2012/06/dangerous-interventions-mms-and-autism.html
11. https://www.esdm.co/
12. https://www.youtube.com/watch?v=OjJ-moe4BpQ
13. https://www.youtube.com/watch?v=OjJ-moe4BpQ
14. http://www.hanen.org/Programs/For-Parents/More-Than-Words.aspx
15. https://www.youtube.com/watch?v=W189Mb-2FnM
16. https://pecsusa.com/pecs/
17. http://www.autismprthelp.com/about-prt.php
18. https://www.youtube.com/watch?v=GGrkZ6UBCJk)
19. http://www.halo-soma.org/learning.php?sess_id=1c82407c837295968cbe7df65475541b
20. https://www.youtube.com/watch?v=6c05Qq5WQew
21. http://www.randrforautism.com/
22. https://www.rdiconnect.com/about-rdi/
23. https://www.youtube.com/watch?v=b-5B0wbjr5s
24. http://scerts.com/
25. https://www.understood.org/en/learning-attention-issues/treatments-approaches/therapies/sensory-integration-therapy-what-you-need-to-know
26. https://www.autismparentingmagazine.com/help-kids-with-autism-everyday
27. https://www.autismtreatmentcenter.org/contents/about_son-rise/what_is_the_son-rise_program.php
28. https://www.youtube.com/watch? v=r5xjc3GUMFg
29. https://earguru.in/en/blogs/speech-therapy/what-is-speech-therapy/
30. https://teacch.com/about-us/
31. https://www.youtube.com/watch?v=ddGLJ2r4rcw

# 3. WHICH PROFESSIONALS MIGHT HELP US?

1. https://www.asha.org/public/speech/development/chart
2. https:// www.asha.org/public/speech/development/Speech-and-Language
3. https://youtu.be/rUGLihrh4EI

# 4. WHAT SHOULD I NOT DO?

1. https://www.washingtonpost.com/news/inspired-life/wp/2018/02/27/bystanders-were-horrified-but-my-son-has-autism-and-i-was-desperate/?utm_term=.aa6204bb5a40
2. http://thesubjectsupposedtoknow.us/terrible-autism-mom-anecdotes-in-the-washington-post/
3. https://somegirlwithabraid.wordpress.com/2018/02/28/autistic-moments-aversions-and-sensitivities/
4. https://notanautismmom.com/2019/05/29/events-one/?fbclid=IwAR14g9CtMa_Ue0Kxv_YzJ7Ac6h-l_ZrwXGGTJc2ruF9hOXFOscWUp2AWmI2A
5. https://us8.campaign-archive.com/?u=4a95c45e015f2b5e28f4df18e&id=9b7ba0be8c

# 5. WHY DID THIS HAPPEN TO US?

1. http://www.our-kids.org/Archives/Holland.html
2. https://www.ncbi.nlm.nih.gov/pmc/articles/PMC3513682/
3. https://genetics.thetech.org/original_news/news49

## 6. SHOULD WE TELL HIM HE HAS AUTISM/IS AUTISTIC?

1. https://www.amazon.com/Freaks-Geeks-Asperger-Syndrome-Adolescence/dp/1843100983
2. https://www.facebook.com/groups/autisminclusivity/
3. https://www.amazon.com/Superflex-Superhero-Social-Thinking-Curriculum/dp/0979292247
4. https://www.youtube.com/watch?v=cJcVMqKcIhc&feature=player_embedded

## 7. PERSON WITH AUTISM OR AUTISTIC PERSON?

1. https://www.cdc.gov/ncbddd/disabilityandhealth/pdf/disabilityposter_photos.pdf
2. https://www.disabilityisnatural.com/people-first-language.html
3. https://www.youtube.com/watch?v=oFGByJN7I5Y
4. https://www.identityfirstautistic.org/
5. https://autisticadvocacy.org/about-asan/identity-first-language/
6. https://adayinourshoes.com/people-first-language/
7. https://news.northeastern.edu/2018/07/12/unpacking-the-debate-over-person-first-vs-identity-first-language-in-the-autism-community/
8. https://themighty.com/2015/08/should-you-use-person-first-or-identity-first-language2/
9. https://youtu.be/YVPjMfgjmU4
10. https://youtu.be/oDnQFQFQ8ec

## 8. WILL HE GROW OUT OF IT?

1. https://theaspergian.com/2019/04/24/ten-things-we-love-about-being-autistic/

# NOTES

## 9. WHAT IS IT WITH THIS SENSORY STUFF?

1. https://www.understood.org/en/learning-attention-issues/treatments-approaches/therapies/download-sample-sensory-diet
2. https://swishforfish.com/pages/nlc-sensory-learning-profile
3. https://www.sensory-processing-disorder.com/adult-SPD-checklist.html
4. https://www.sensory-processing-disorder.com/sensory-processing-disorder-checklist.html
5. http://www.sspcmaine.com/forms/Sensory%20Profile.pdf
6. https://sensationalbrain.com/free-resources/

## 12. OLFACTORY SENSE

1. https://www.amazon.com/Crayola-Silly-Scents-Twistables-Stinky/dp/B07NX8FRD7/

## 13. VISUAL SENSE

1. https://www.understood.org/en/learning-attention-issues/treatments-approaches/educational-strategies/universal-design-for-learning-what-it-is-and-how-it-works
2. https://www.aap.org/en-us/about-the-aap/aap-press-room/Pages/American-Academy-of-Pediatrics-Announces-New-Recommendations-for-Childrens-Media-Use.aspx
3. https://www.sleepfoundation.org/articles/how-blue-light-affects-kids-sleep

## 14. GUSTATORY SENSE

1. https://sosapproach-conferences.com

## 15. VESTIBULAR SYSTEM

1. https://neuroscientificallychallenged.com/blog/know-your-brain-vestibular-system
2. https://www.amazon.com/Hokki-Stool-15-Blue/dp/B005JZ6YLK

## 16. PROPRIOCEPTION

1. http://sensory-processing.middletownautism.com/sensory-strategies/strategies-according-to-sense/proprioceptive/
2. https://www.andnextcomesl.com/2015/06/heavy-work-activities-for-kids.html

## 17. INTEROCEPTION

1. https://www.understood.org/en/learning-attention-issues/child-learning-disabilities/sensory-processing-issues/interoception-and-sensory-processing-issues-what-you-need-to-know
2. https://copingskillsforkids.com/deep-breathing-exercises-for-kids.
3. https://childhood101.com/fun-breathing-exercises-for-kids/.
4. https://www.mother.ly/parenting/3-breathing-exercises-to-calm-kids-of-all-ages.
5. https://www.autism-society.org/news/ask-expert-kelly-mahler-ms-otrl/.
6. https://www.youtube.com/watch?v=VU9CqbhmBWQ.
7. https://youtu.be/1XJX2MlzTd0
8. https://www.spdstar.org/sites/default/files/file-attachments/Interoception_Info_Sheet_7_17_0.pdf

# 19. HOW DO YOU WORK WITH YOUR SCHOOL?

1. *Autism Goes to School* https://books2read.com/AutismGoestoSchool.
2. *Autism Runs Away* https://books2readcom./AutismRunsAway.

# 20. WILL HE EVER TALK?

1. https://find.asha.org/pro#f:@Provider=%5BSpeech-Language%20Pathologist%5D.
2. https://www.sac-oac.ca/find-speech-language-pathologist-or-audiologist-service.
3. https://www.therapy-directory.org.uk/articles/speech-and-language-therapy.html.
4. https://www.asha.org/public/speech/development/chart/
5. https://www.youtube.com/watch?v=4c5_3wqZ3Lk&t=335s
6. https://www.youtube.com/watch?v=4c5_3wqZ3Lk&t=335s
7. http://www.cnn.com/2007/HEALTH/02/21/autism.amanda/index.html
8. https://www.huffpost.com/entry/carly-fleischmann-carlys-cafe_n_3492008
9. http://idoinautismland.com/
10. https://the-art-of-autism.com/tito-autism-is-my-destiny/
11. https://www.thoughtco.com/theory-of-mind-4165566
12. https://pdfs.semanticscholar.org/8e05/0a823df6aca24aab2cf0ed5855e546974164.pdf

# 21. WHAT IF HE NEVER TALKS?

1. Picture cards available at http://do2learn.com/picturecards/overview.htm

## NOTES

2. https://carolgraysocialstories.com/social-stories/what-is-it/
3. https://www.assistiveware.com/products/proloquo2go
4. Sample communication apps https://www.friendshipcircle.org/blog/2011/02/07/7-assistive-communication-apps-in-the-ipad-app-store/

    Assistive communication apps for kids https://www.speechandlanguagekids.com/aac-apps-review/

    Android apps for social needs kids https://www.eastersealstech.com/2015/07/01/6-android-apps-for-special-needs/

    Free and inexpensive communication apps http://www.centralcoastchildrensfoundation.org/draft/wp-content/uploads/2012/03/FreeandInexpensiveAACAppsFinal.pdf

    Alternate and augmentative apps for iPad https://www.lifewire.com/top-alternative-and-augmentative-communication-198828
5. Pictello social story app https://www.assistiveware.com/products/pictello
6. Demonstration of Pictello https://www.youtube.com/watch?v=9B1fAaAS3N4&t=38s
7. Does using AAC impede the child developing speech? https://www.asha.org/PRPSpecificTopic.aspx?folderid=8589942773&section=Key_Issues#AAC_Myths_and_Realities
8. Positive effects of AAC https://www.assistiveware.com/learn-aac/roadblock-aac-will-stop-a-person-from-learning-to-speak
9. Dynavox touch-based speech generator https://www.tobiidynavox.com/en-US/devices/multi-access-devices/i-110-na/
10. One site for information on American Sign Language http://www.lifeprint.com
11. https://www.british-sign.co.uk/what-is-british-sign-language/
12. https://www.makaton.org/aboutMakaton/
13. https://www.babysignlanguage.com/basics/?v=3e8d115eb4b3

14. https://www.youtube.com/watch?v=YjYbopUNQEw
15. https://www.asha.org/public/speech/disorders/childhood-apraxia-of-speech/
16. https://www.youtube.com/watch?v=cEOy3APLA-g
17. http://videos.apraxia-kids.org/WhatIsApraxiaPamphlet.mp4
18. https://researchautism.org/i-have-nonverbal-autism-heres-what-i-want-you-to-know/
19. http://idoinautismland.com/?p=843
20. http://kayliespeaks.blogspot.com/2018/
21. https://returningjames.com/2018/06/
22. https://the-art-of-autism.com/emma-an-autistic-girl-whose-body-and-mouth-words-do-not-always-pay-attention-to-her-bright-and-wise-mind/
23. https://monadelahooke.com/being-nonverbal-doesnt-mean-i-cant-think/
24. http://www.goldenhatfoundation.org/about-us/blog/125-golden-hat-foundation-blog-70211
25. https://www.youtube.com/watch?v=xMBzJleeOno&t=164s
26. https://www.youtube.com/watch?v=qn70gPukdtY&t=6s

## 22. WHAT DOES MINIMALLY VERBAL MEAN?

1. An autistic opinion on echolalia https://www.youtube.com/watch?v=8OeyOMrp68w
2. Ask an autistic – what is echolalia https://www.youtube.com/watch?v=ome-95iHtB0.

## 23. WHAT IF HE TALKS TOO MUCH?

1. Small Talk Can Loom Large: Teaching Your Child the Flow of Conversation https://autismawarenesscentre.com/small-talk-can-loom-large-teaching-child-flow-conversation/.

2. Six Tips for Teaching Conversation Skills With Visual Strategies https://campussuite-storage.s3.amazonaws.com/prod/11162/b2004386-1ca3-11e6-b537-22000bd8490f/1687658/c27f3ea2-ff6c-11e7-a236-0a3960e4824a/file/conversationskills.pdf.
3. Teaching Conversation Skills https://www.autismoutreach.ca/elearning/social-skills/teaching-conversation-skills.
4. Teaching Conversational Skills https://theautismhelper.com/teaching-conversation-skills/.
5. How to Teach Conversation Skills to Students with Autism Teaching Conversation Skills to Students with Autism ... - ASHA https://www.asha.org/Events/convention/handouts/2014/1651-Muller/.

## 27. IS HE HIGH OF LOW FUNCTIONING?

1. Why Intelligence Scores Do Not Predict Success for autistic Adults https://www.spectrumnews.org/opinion/viewpoint/intelligence-scores-not-predict-success-autistic-adults/.
2. What About Functioning https://drexel.edu/autismoutcomes/blog/overview/2015/September/What-About-Functioning/
3. Functioning Labels: Why You Shouldn't Be Using Them https://www.theautisticadvocate.com/2017/10/functioning-labels-why-you-shouldnt-be.html
4. Please Listen to Autistic People https://www.msn.com/en-us/health/wellness/this-autism-awareness-month-please-listen-to-autistic-people/ar-BBW3dDD

## 28. IS HE LAZY?

1. Kidspiration http://www.inspiration.com/go/kidsmaps.
2. Mind mapping concept https://litemind.com/what-is-mind-mapping/.
3. 8 Free Mind-Mapping Tools https://www.makeuseof.com/tag/8-free-mind-map-tools-best-use/.
4. MindMup https://www.mindmup.com/.
5. Best Mind-Mapping Software of 2019 https://financesonline.com/mind-mapping/.
6. https://www.youtube.com/watch?v=3StCt1FK4Pc&t=47s

## 29. WILL HE BE ABLE TO LIVE ON HIS OWN?

1. Stephen Shore https://www.youtube.com/watch?v=0teFbz4TB-A.
2. Carly Fleischmann https://www.chatelaine.com/living/real-life-stories/my-daughters-severe-autism-and-how-she-found-her-voice/.
3. Amanda Baggs https://well.blogs.nytimes.com/2008/02/28/the-language-of-autism/.

## 30. WILL HE BE ABLE TO HOLD DOWN A JOB?

1. Amanda's videos https://www.youtube.com/watch?v=4c5_3wqZ3Lk&t=287s.
2. Carly's videos https://www.youtube.com/watch?v=xMBzJleeOno&t=84s.
3. Chef Tom Dickinson https://www.youtube.com/watch?v=Wv7HbBe86mc.
4. EveryDay Aspie https://everydayaspie.wordpress.com/2019/06/04/ask-an-autistic-10-

considerations-you-should-know-now-not-tomorrow/.
5. 10 Considerations for the Autistic Workforce https://everydayaspie.wordpress.com/2019/06/04/ask-an-autistic-10-considerations-you-should-know-now-not-tomorrow/.
6. Chef Chris Fisher https://gossipgist.com/chris-fischer.

www.ingramcontent.com/pod-product-compliance
Lightning Source LLC
Chambersburg PA
CBHW020405040426
42333CB00055B/470